CARMARTHENSHIRE'S MILITARY HERITAGE

DEAN HOLLANDS

I0806086

AMBERLEY

This book is dedicated to the memory of all those whose actions and deeds have created Carmarthenshire's military heritage, and to all those who unyieldingly continue to preserve it.

First published 2024

Amberley Publishing
The Hill, Stroud,
Gloucestershire, GL5 4EP

www.amberley-books.com

Copyright © Dean Hollands, 2024

The right of Dean Hollands to be identified as the Author of this work has been asserted in accordance with the Copyright, Designs and Patents Act 1988.

All rights reserved. No part of this book may be reprinted or reproduced or utilised in any form or by any electronic, mechanical or other means, now known or hereafter invented, including photocopying and recording, or in any information storage or retrieval system, without the permission in writing from the Publishers.

ISBN: 978 1 3981 1676 4 (print)
ISBN: 978 1 3981 1677 1 (ebook)

British Library Cataloguing in Publication Data.
A catalogue record for this book is available from the British Library.

Typeset in 10pt on 13pt Celeste.
Origination by Amberley Publishing.
Printed in the UK.

Contents

Introduction 4

1 Invaders and Conquerors 5

2 Earthworks and Forts 15

3 Castles and Bunkers 23

4 Riots and Revolts 40

5 Adventurers and Explorers 52

6 Heroes and Heroism 61

7 Munitions and Explosives 73

8 Monuments and Memorials 81

Acknowledgements 95

About the Author 96

Introduction

Inhabited since prehistoric times, the county name of Carmarthenshire, 'Sir Gaerfyrddin' in Welsh, only came into existence during the thirteenth century, when Edward I made it a shire. Known as 'The Garden of Wales', Carmarthenshire is a county blessed with natural beauty and a military heritage as diverse as it is ancient. A heritage forged by bloodthirsty raiders and invaders intent on murder, massacre, subjugation, and conquest. Despite the passage of time, the heritage of many of those military encounters remains today, besides the many monuments and memorials that commemorate and remember the people, places and events that have shaped that heritage. The remains of Iron Age camps, Roman forts, Norman castles, Second World War fortifications and Cold War bunkers all exist as poignant legacies of the courage, unyielding determination, and sacrifices made by civilians and military personnel who have gallantly served their county and country at home and abroad in times of peace and war. While riots, rebellions and revolts have frequently involved military interventions, the real legacy of the county's military heritage is found in the collective stories, accomplishments, epic endeavours, successes, failures, and sacrifices of its people; distinguished sons and notable daughters, whose watch words courage, endurance, and perseverance reflect perfectly the Welsh patriotic spirit. Their feats of bravery, self-sacrifice, and heroism continue to invigorate and inspire new generations of residents and visitors alike. Such is the extent and diverse nature of Carmarthenshire's military heritage, it is not possible to include or comment in depth on every aspect of that heritage within the pages of this publication. However, this book provides a concise and informative overview of the important military periods in the county's history, as well as the contributions made by those better and lesser-known individuals associated with the county. Signposting the readers to some of the many military locations, key individuals, and events within Carmarthenshire, it is the author's hope that readers will be inspired and intrigued to learn more about the county's military heritage, to explore the sites within this book, discover others, and share those experiences.

Dean Hollands, 2024

1

Invaders and Conquerors

The peoples of Wales are fiercely proud of their cultural heritage. This and their ability to remain a separate nation have been forged through centuries of adversity.

River Drift Man and his successor Stone Age Man were the first invaders of the area known today as Carmarthenshire. They were hunter-gatherers arriving from Europe around 12000 BCE over a land bridge which once connected the two.

What little is known about these people comes from the remains of their skeletons, tools, and weapons unearthed in the county's gravel beds and caves. Both races possessed axes, spears, and knives made from rough unpolished chipped stone. While offering a fleeting insight into their daily lives, how, or how not, they used these as arms is unknown, and much speculation between historians and archaeologists exists over this issue.

Around 5000 BCE, a race of people known as New Stone Man or Iberians arrived in Britain from the Mediterranean. These invaders were farmers in search of fertile rich land who brought with them innovative technologies marking the beginning of Britain's New Stone Age.

Using improved grinding and polishing techniques, the Iberians perfected the art of creating razor sharp-edged tools and weapons, which they used against the tribes of Old Stone Age man. Slowly the Iberian culture became the dominant race across Britain.

Their dominance lasted until around 2000 BCE when the arrival of a second population of farmers heralded the next technological advances in tool and weapon manufacture. These were the Bell Beaker people from Central Europe. Their ancestors had migrated westward from the Eurasian Steppe over many generations, eventually arriving in south-west Wales. Their coming heralded the end of the Stone Age and the beginning of the Bronze Age. A knowledge of metal working processes enabled them to produce superior weapons and farming implements from copper and bronze; although predominately farmers, the Bell Beakers were proficient with bows and slingshot.

Like their predecessors Stone Age Man, it was the Iberians' turn to be disadvantaged and at the mercy of the new invaders. Several hundred years of Bell Beaker migration led to eradication of the Iberians as a dominant race.

With few external influences the Bell Beaker people prospered and expanded their territory. Sporadic inter-tribal rivalries resulted in open warfare and warring factions raided one another. During times of economic hardship or famine war parties from further afield would travel from modern day England, Scotland, and Ireland to raid the rich tribes of Wales. Loss of life through military conflict was minimal compared to the loss of life caused through shortages of food stolen by raiders.

The next major invasion of Wales took place around 800 BCE and heralded the Iron Age as a confederation of Celts from central Europe arrived with advanced knowledge of iron-working technology. Capitalising on this superior metallurgy, the Celts made their presence known through trade, warfare, and land grabbing. They quickly divided up the spoils of military conquests, allocating regions of lands to individual tribes or small confederations of tribes who settled, worked, and fortified their allocated lands.

The names commonly associated with the Iron Age tribes of Britain were given by Roman and Greek scholars and were not necessarily the names used by the tribes, sadly now no longer known. In south-west Wales in what we know today to be the counties of Pembrokeshire, Cardigan and Carmarthenshire the predominating Celtic tribes were the Demetae.

By 400 BCE the use of iron artefacts was common across the British Isles, replacing bronze implements of warfare and peace with iron ones. The Demetae also used their knowledge of metalworking to fortify existing hill forts against tribal raiders and other warring factors. In time the Demetae became powerful and wealthy, expanding across the three modern counties of Pembroke, Cardigan, and Carmarthen. Like the other four nation tribes of Wales, the Silures, Ordovices, Deceangli, and the Cornovii, they thrived commercially, dominating, and defending their territories against regional and local raiders. Neither their military prowess nor their commercial influence could stop the next invaders conquering Wales.

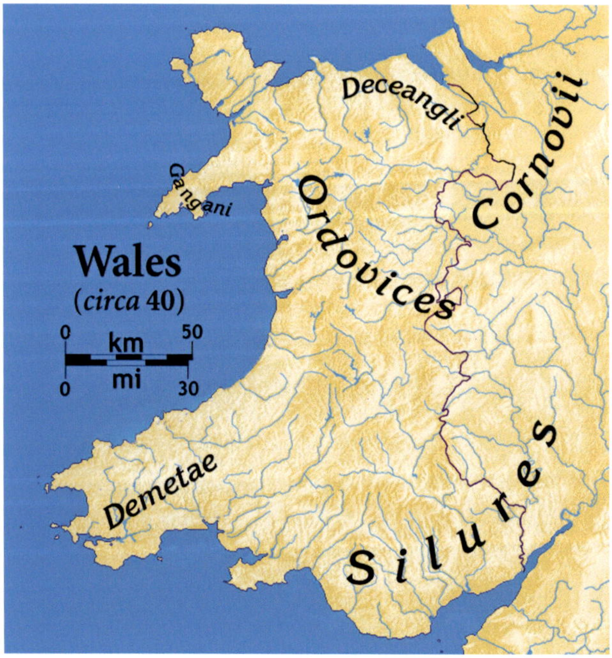

John Edward Lloyd's 1912 *History of Wales* (2 vols). (CC BY-SA 3.0)

When a Roman army sent by Emperor Claudius arrived in 48 CE, their military force, and unequalled discipline, proved no match for the tribes of Wales. Their intent was to subdue the tribes of Wales in search of mineral wealth. General Publius Ostorius Scapula's campaign began in the north-east with an attack against the Deceangli, who surrendered with little resistance. He then moved east and attacked the Demetae's neighbours the Silures, and finally the Ordovices in the north. Scapula's army met fierce resistance from these tribes; their hill forts and strongholds repelled attacks and the tribes remained defiant.

For many years the Silures and Ordovices successfully waged a guerrilla war against the Romans. It is not known if the tribes were defeated or came to a peace agreement, but both were eventually conquered. The Demetae did not oppose Rome, and their conquest was a peaceful affair, which allowed them to keep their tribal name. The Demetae were the only tribe who survived the Roman conquest and occupation period with their homeland and identity intact until the Middle Ages.

During their occupation, Romans mined gold and other minerals, governed, collected taxes, and opened commercial links until they abandoned the region in 383 CE. Their withdrawal left a void in power that saw the land ravished and its people attacked by a succession of raiders and invaders striving to fill the gap.

Wales did not escape the brutality of Viking raids which plagued other parts of the British Isles. From 850 to 870 CE, the territory formerly occupied by the Demetae, known at the time as Deheubarth, was raided annually by large numbers of warring Vikings. Raiding became sporadic until 952 CE when annual raids resumed until 1000 CE.

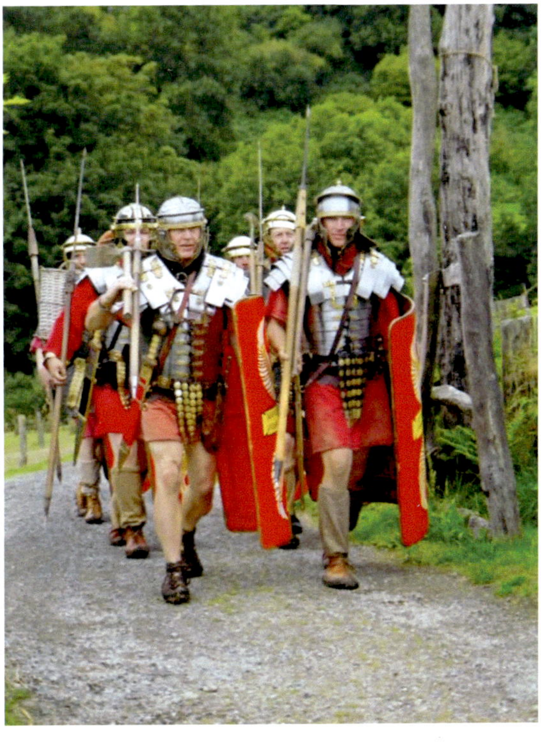

Roman re-enactors. (HP)

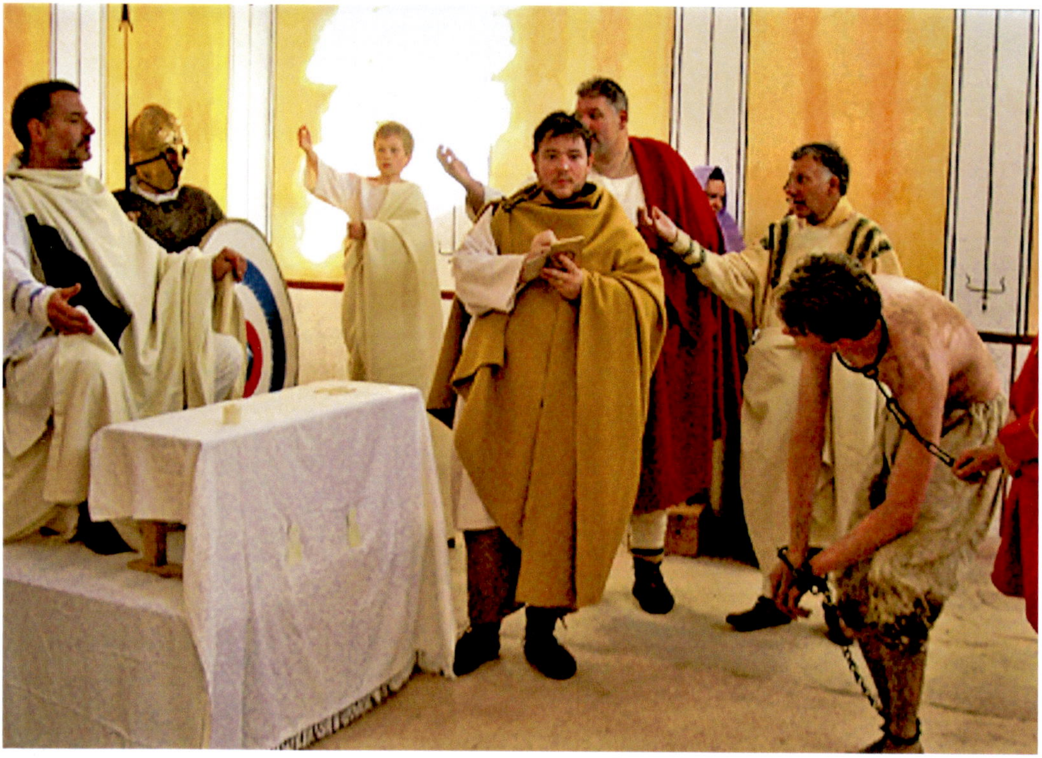

Roman re-enactors. (NS)

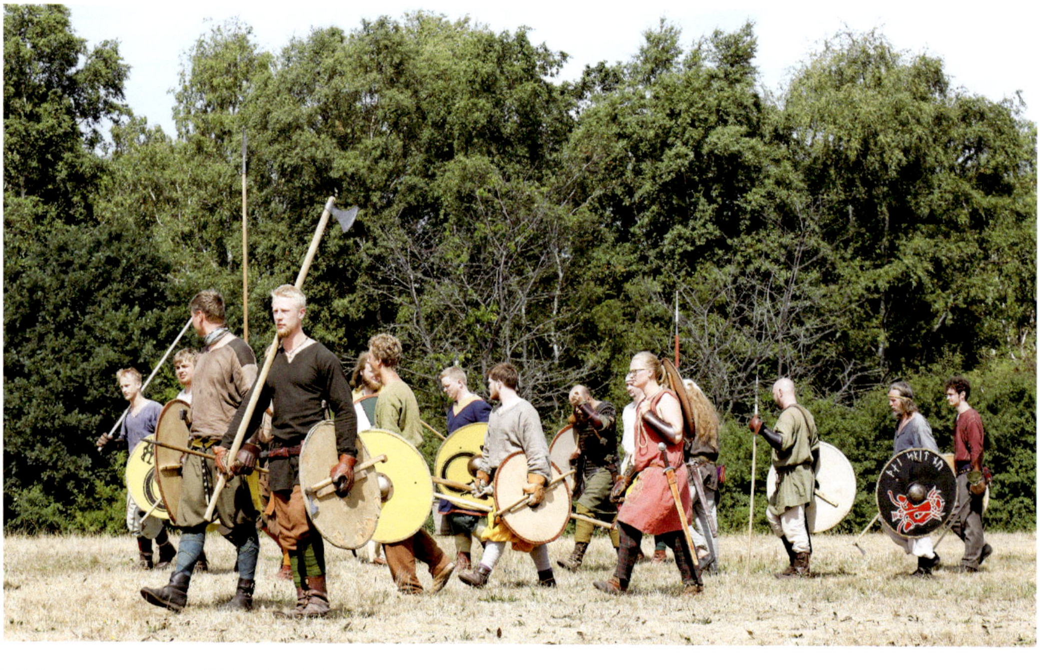

Viking re-enactors. (Ricochet69)

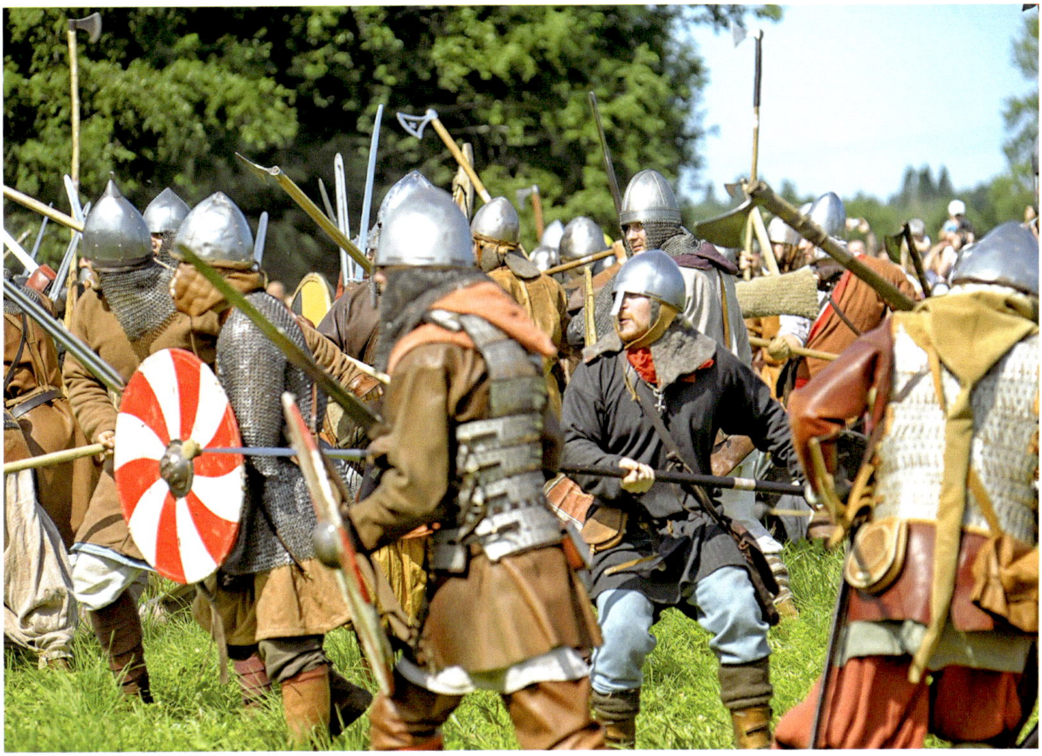

Viking re-enactors. (PK)

Norsemen from the Hiberno-Norse kingdoms of Dublin and Limerick inflicted most coastal raids, while other raiders travelled from England. In 1042, near Carmarthen, King Hywel ap Edwin of Deheubarth was victorious over a horde of Viking marauders. The following year King Gruffydd ap Llywelyn defeated King Hywel ap Edwin in battle at Carmarthen, who, having fled Wales, enlisted the services of Irish Viking mercenaries to regain his throne. Hywel returned with a fleet of twenty longships but was killed in battle near the mouth of the river Towy. Viking incursions continued across the county until the arrival of the next foreign force to conquer Wales.

The Norman invasion of Wales was a slow affair. In 1081, William the Conqueror, King of England, had no intention of conquering Wales. He wanted to ensure the stability of his frontier border, so gave lands along the Welsh border to his strongest and most loyal barons. These barons encouraged their followers to move west into Welsh territory.

The Normans had a military advantage over the Welsh. Norman knights were better armoured and horsed, and erected castles to keep their territory secure.

When William died in 1087, his son King Henry I encouraged large-scale Norman settlement in south Wales. Lands were stolen and people suppressed, yet Wales remained unconquered until Edward I became king of England. Edward disliked all Celts, and particularly Llewelyn ap Gruffydd, who had taken to calling himself the Prince of Wales. In 1277, Edward conquered Wales through three major campaigns and on a scale the Welsh could not hope to match, completing his conquest in 1283.

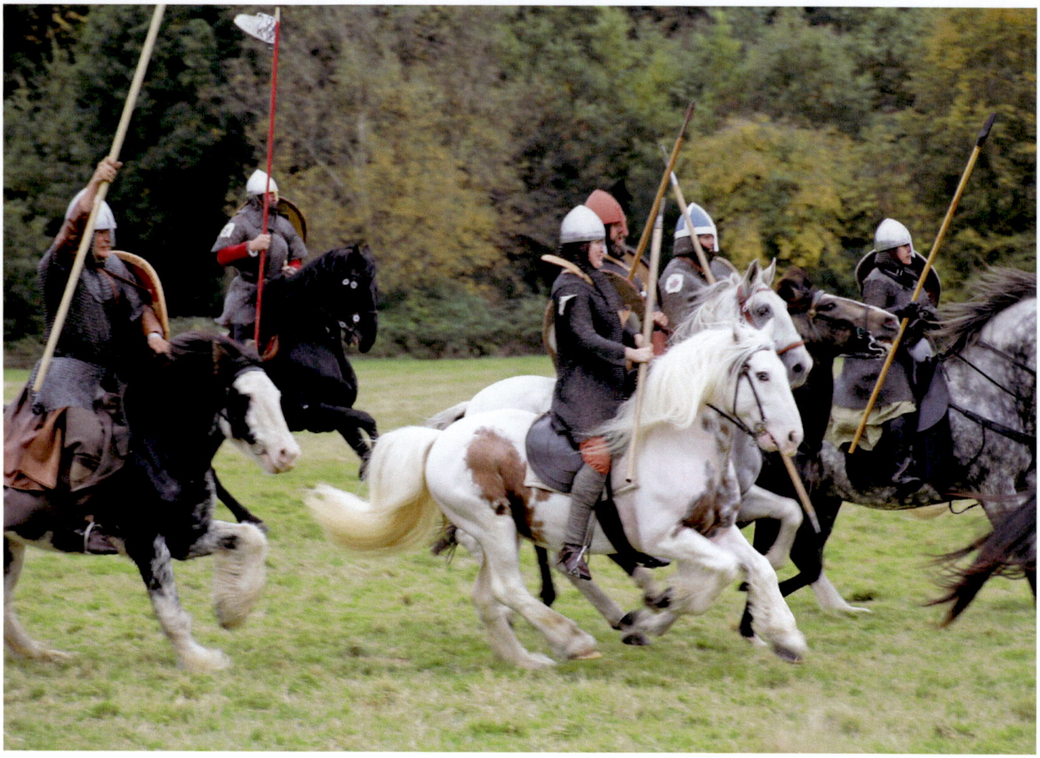

Norman re-enactors. (CM)

The threat of major invasion subsided under English control, and it wouldn't be resurrected until the start of the Second World War. When France fell in June 1940, Germany's Führer and Supreme Commander, Adolf Hitler, made it clear that any rejection of his peace settlement would result in the destruction of Britain and its empire. When it was rejected, Hitler activated Operation *Sea Lion*, the invasion of Britain. Vital to his invasion plan was the destruction of the Royal Air Force's (RAF) pilots, planes, and airfields, to gain German air supremacy over Britain and its coastal waters.

One of the largest RAF defences in Carmarthenshire was the station at Pembrey. Constructed in 1936, Pembrey was a RAF training facility for anti-aircraft gunners of No. 280 Ground Defence Squadron, becoming No. 2 Air Armament School in 1939. In June 1940, France had fallen, and the Battle of Britain was about to commence; Pembrey came under the command and control of No. 10 Group, Fighter Command. Pembrey's main function was to provide rest and recuperation for pilots involved in sustained active service.

On 18 June, the Spitfires of No. 92 (East India) Squadron began operating out of Pembrey. Having seen service during the evacuation of Dunkirk the squadron flew convoys around the Welsh coast while their exhausted pilots recuperated, and they recruited pilots to replace those injured at Dunkirk. In September 1940 they were replaced by No. 79 Squadron flying Hurricanes, their pilots veterans of the Battle for France and the ongoing Battle of Britain.

A small flight from No. 14 Operational Training Unit, equipped with Handley Page Hampden and Hereford twin-engine medium bombers, were also stationed at Pembrey. Their job was to train bomber crews in night flying.

February 1941 saw the formation of No. 316 'Warszawski' Squadron, a Polish fighter squadron flying Hurricanes. The squadron was drawn from members of the 1st Warsaw Air Regiment, pilots who had fled Poland following Germany's invasion in 1939. Already providing defensive cover across the south-west of England, they began offensive sweeps over northern France in August 1940.

On 17 April 1941, another Hurricane squadron, No. 32, arrived, and in June the RAF's Training Command took over from Fighter Command. During the war Pembrey lost many aircraft and aircrew in flying accidents, and many of them are buried in the cemetery at nearby St Illtyd churchyard (see chapter eight).

Between 9 July 1940 and 21 February 1941, Llangennech, Llanelli, Pembrey, Kidwelly and many other Carmarthenshire villages and factories were damaged by German bombers and lives were lost. RAF Pembrey and the nearby Royal Ordnance Factory were major targets for German bombers and the area experienced a great deal of enemy action.

One unusual event occurred on 23 June 1942, when German Luftwaffe pilot Oberleutnant Armin Faber unexpectedly landed at RAF Pembrey. He was adjutant to the commander of Luftwaffe Jagdgeschwader III JG2 in northern France. Faber had special permission to fly combat missions with a squadron flying Focke-Wulf 190 (FW-190) fighters. Recently

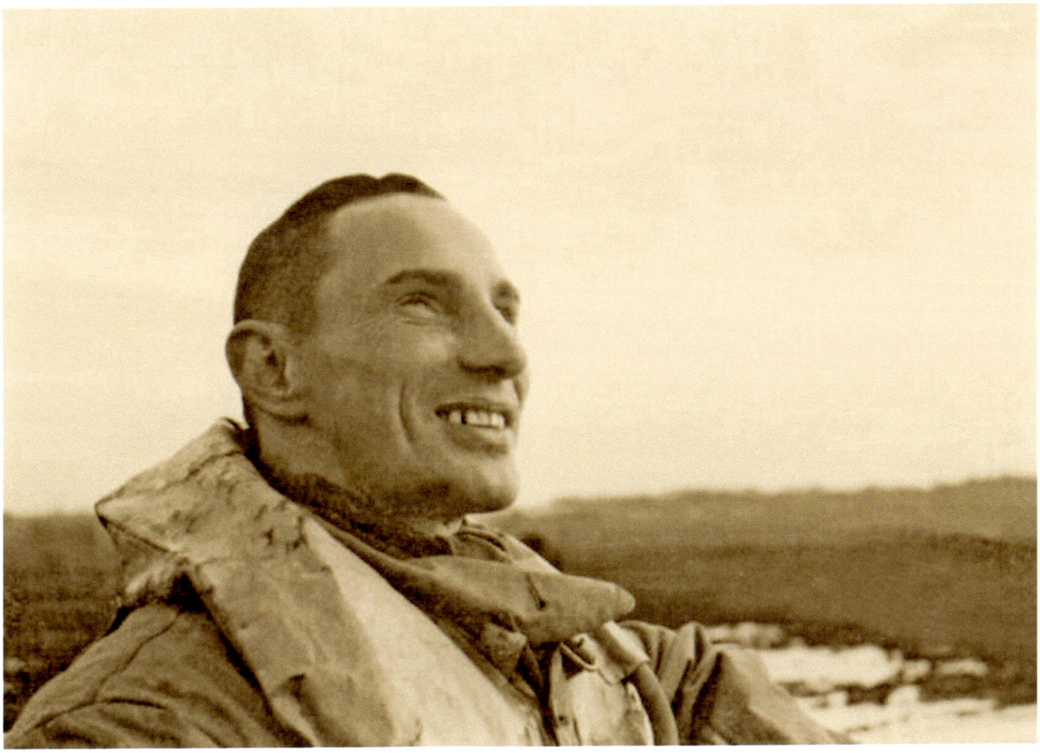

Oberleutnant Armin Faber. (DD)

deployed to front line units, the FW-190, was so superior to Allied planes that plans were underway to launch a commando raid on a French airfield to seize one for evaluation.

Spitfires escorting a force of twelve RAF Douglas Boston planes returning from a bombing raid engaged Faber's squadron. Faber was attacked, pursued, and became disorientated. Mistaking the Bristol Channel for the English Channel, he flew north instead of south. Out of fuel and believing South Wales to be France, he headed for the nearest airfield.

Tipping his wings in victory, Faber landed at RAF Pembrey and was immediately captured, along with his aircraft, by duty pilot Sergeant Jeffreys, who, having ran from the control tower, climbed onto Faber's aircraft as it taxied and using his Very pistol (flare gun) forced him to stop.

No. 1 Air Gunners School flying Bristol Blenheim, Avro Anson, and Vickers Wellington medium bombers were the station's longest residents. Following the war and until its closure in 1957, Pembrey was home to No. 233 Operational Conversion Unit, which flew de Havilland Vampire and Hawker Hunter jet fighters.

During 1997 to 1998, Pembrey was used by civil aircraft. Despite extensive redevelopment, the landing area layout and some original RAF buildings survive, including a rare dome trainer building for training anti-aircraft gunners. Forty-four dome trainers were built between 1939 and 1945, although today only six remain. The example in Pembrey is the only one left in Wales.

The last military invasion of Carmarthenshire was not hostile. It began in late 1943, when in advance of Operation *Overlord*, the codename for the Allied invasion of Europe, thousands of men from the United States Army's 28th Infantry Division arrived. Destined for Normandy, they were billeted in tents, huts, and buildings throughout the county.

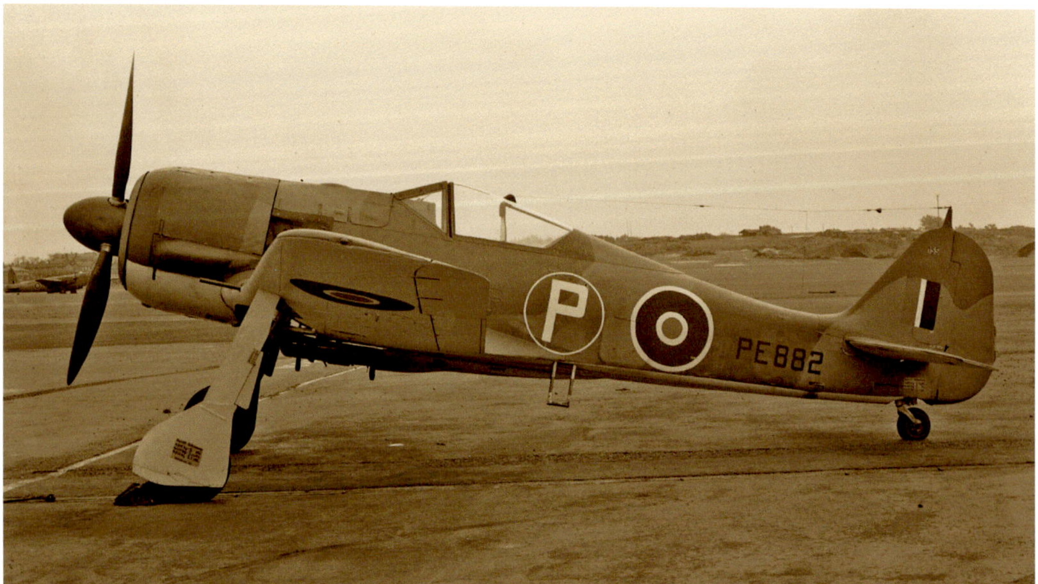

Faber's FW-190 British Livery. (FAST)

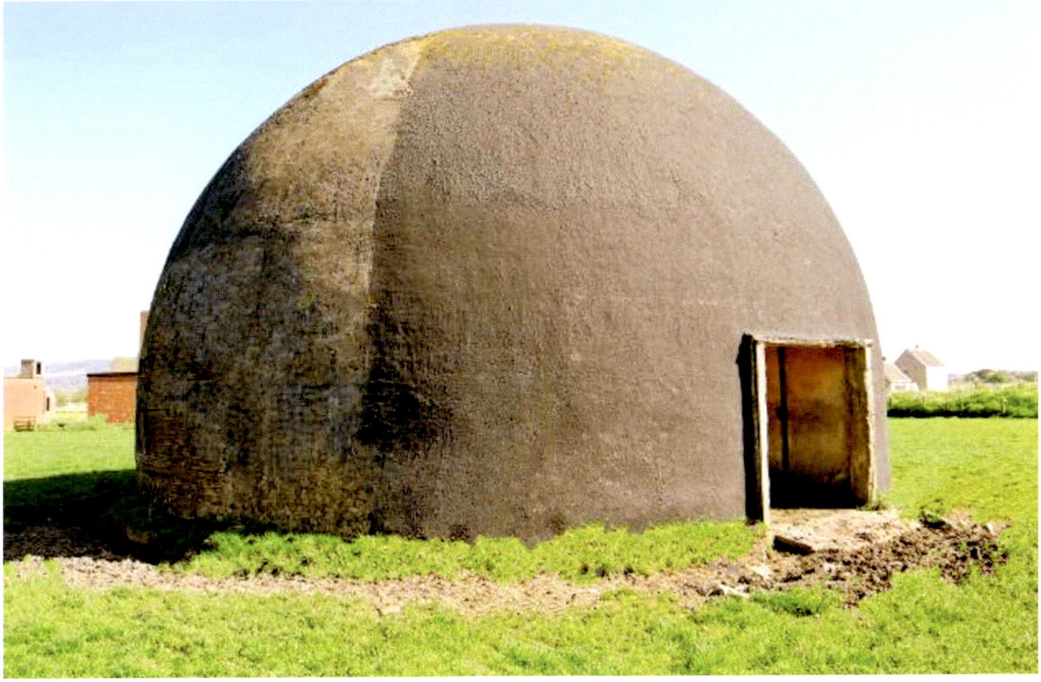

Pembrey Gunnery Training Dome.

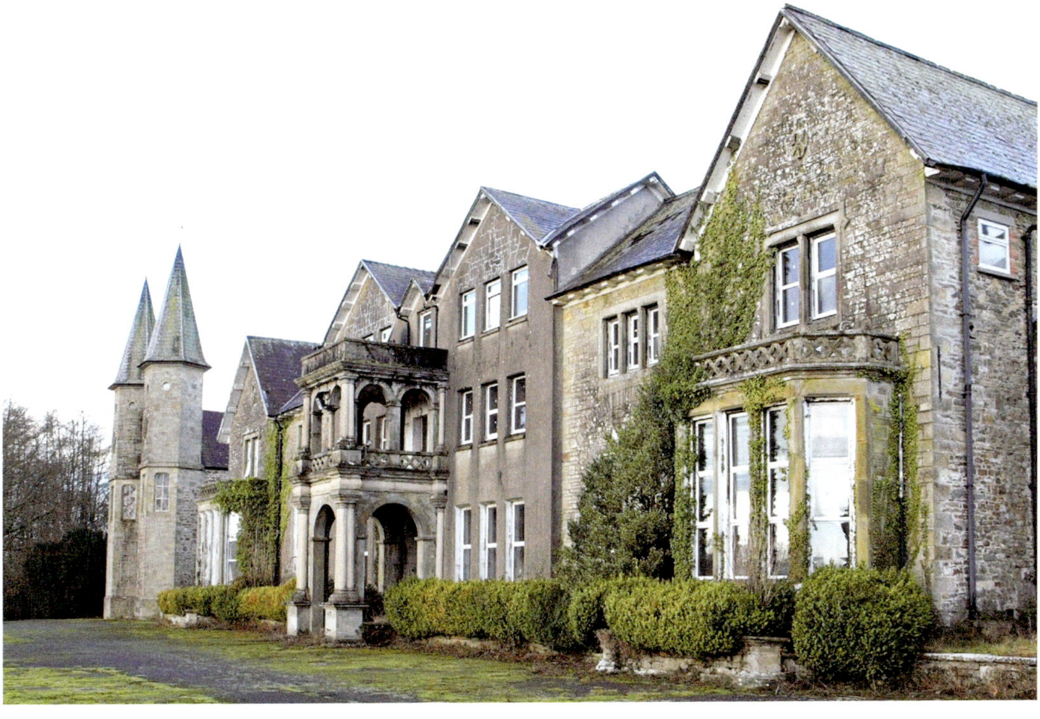

Highmead House.

The 112th Infantry Regiment Headquarters, 103rd Medical Battalion and 1st Battalion were located at Highmead House, Llanybydder. Following the war, the house became a school and in 1998 an Islamic college where Michael Adebowale studied. Adebowale went on to take part in a terrorist attack near army barracks in Woolwich, South East London, on 22 May 2013, during which he murdered Fusilier Lee Rigby.

The 2nd Battalion was based at Ystrad Camp, Carmarthen, and the 3rd Battalion was camped across Kidwelly, Pembrey, and Burry Port.

Drefach Felindre was home to the 109th Battalion's field artillery and their anti-tank company were concealed in the woods at Treglog above Abergorlech. The Division's 103rd Engineer Combat Battalion was located at Abermarlais Park in the Towy Valley between Llandeilo and Llandovery, and between March and May 1944 the American 38th Infantry Regiment's headquarters were at Broomhill House, Kidwelly.

2

Earthworks and Forts

The ancient landscape of Carmarthenshire is strewn with the remnants of hill forts, castles, fortified buildings, and military establishments, the result of a perfect storm of military aggression, subjugation, conquest and subsequent advances in science and technology creating defensive fortifications each bigger, better, and stronger than those that came before.

The earliest defensive structures were Neolithic hill forts built during the Bronze and Iron Age. Constructed at strategic locations, many sites were repeatedly attacked, occupied, and redeveloped by raiders, invaders, and forces intent on conquest. As a result, they contain evidence of military occupation from the pre-Bronze Age through to the Roman era and beyond.

Bronze Age enclosures were surrounded by one or more ditches and protected by steep earthen ramparts. People entered via walkways cutting through the ramparts that bridged the ditches at either end of the enclosure, where giant gates controlled access. Hill forts were symbols of wealth and military power and when not functioning as fortifications were used for storing crops, sheltering from extreme weather, and for social and religious gatherings.

Celtic invaders, arriving in 550 BCE, used their new Iron Age technologies to expand existing enclosures by making the ditches deeper, reinforcing earthen walls with timber and flint, and excavating soil and chalk to make the ramparts higher before adding wooden walls.

Eighty Iron Age forts have been recorded across the county. These once impressive fortifications with their imposing gateways, palisades and earthworks dominated the landscape, affording protection and security. Today now reduced to low banks, shallow ditches, or fragments of stonework, they remain in various states of erosion and disrepair.

Erected during the early Bronze Age, Carn Goch, in the Brecon Beacons National Park, high above the Tywi Valley, is one of the largest and most extraordinary hill fort complexes in Wales. It is the site of two forts: Y Gaer Fach (the small fort) and Y Gaer Fawr (the large fort). Y Gaer Fawr covers 11.2 hectares and has six separate entrances marked by pairs of large upright stones that controlled access to the fort. Y Gaer Fach covers 1.5 hectares. Between 47 and 78 CE the camps protected two positions on adjacent hilltops. Both ramparts are visible, as is the vast burial cairn which gives the larger fort its name.

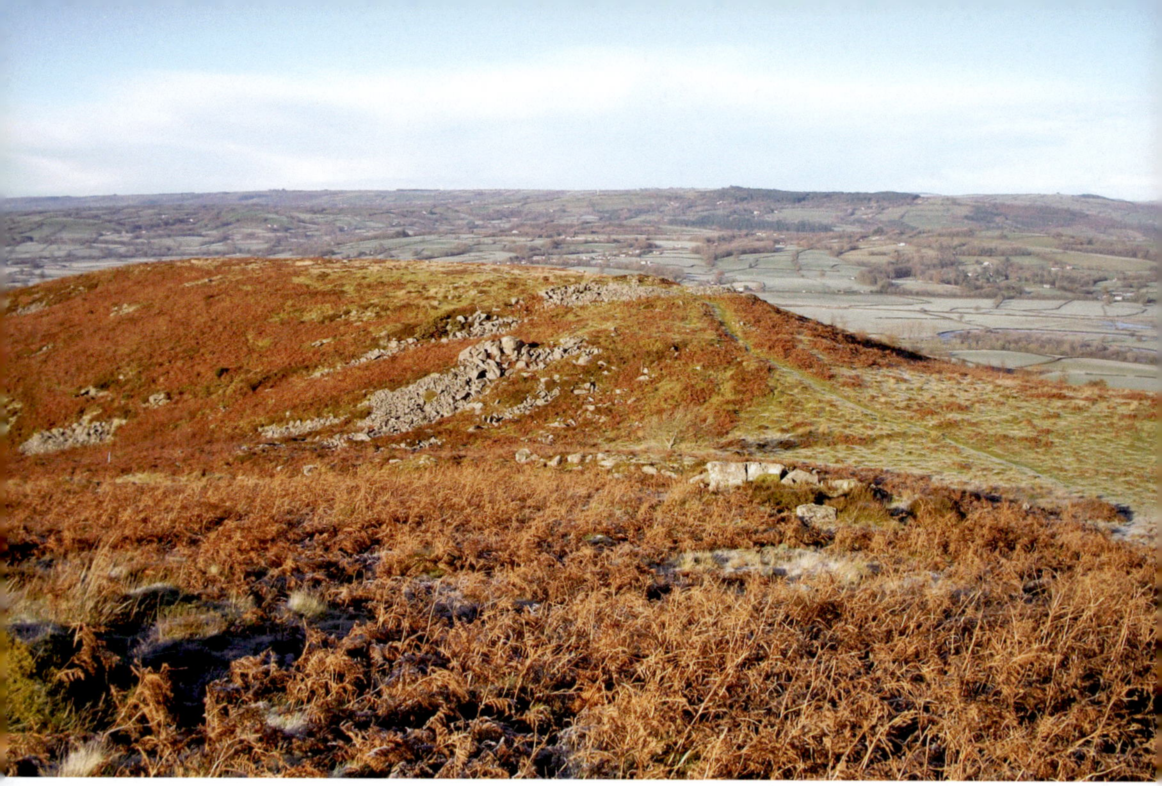

Y Gaer Fawr from Y Gaer Fach.

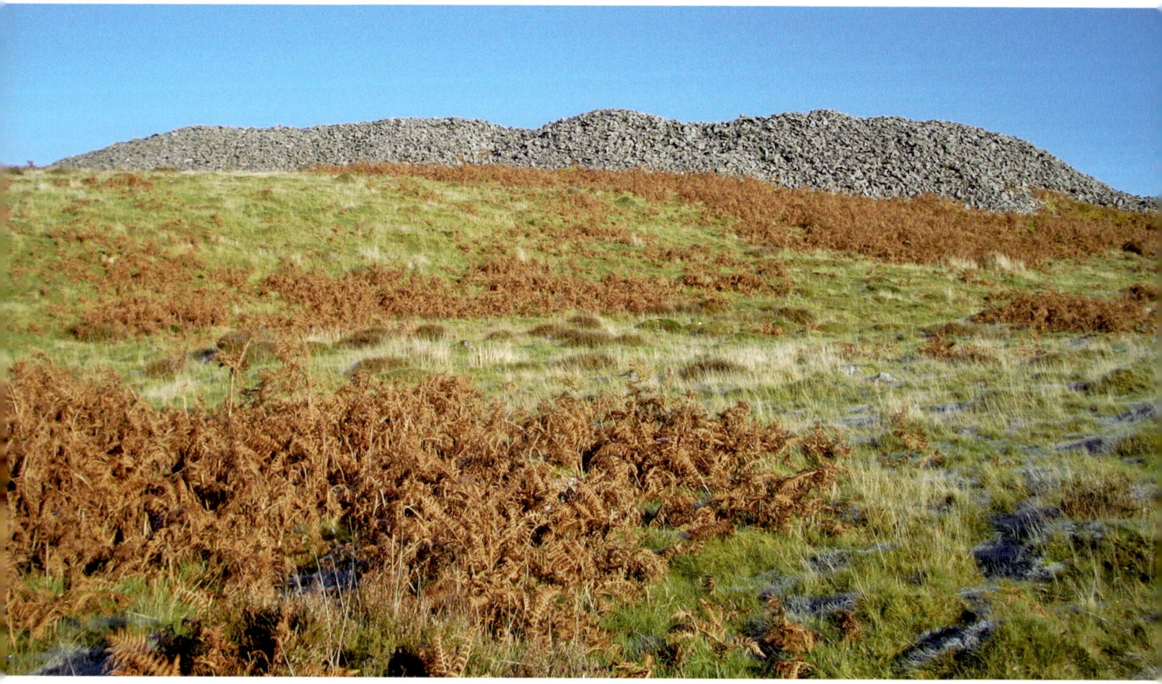

Y Garn Goch.

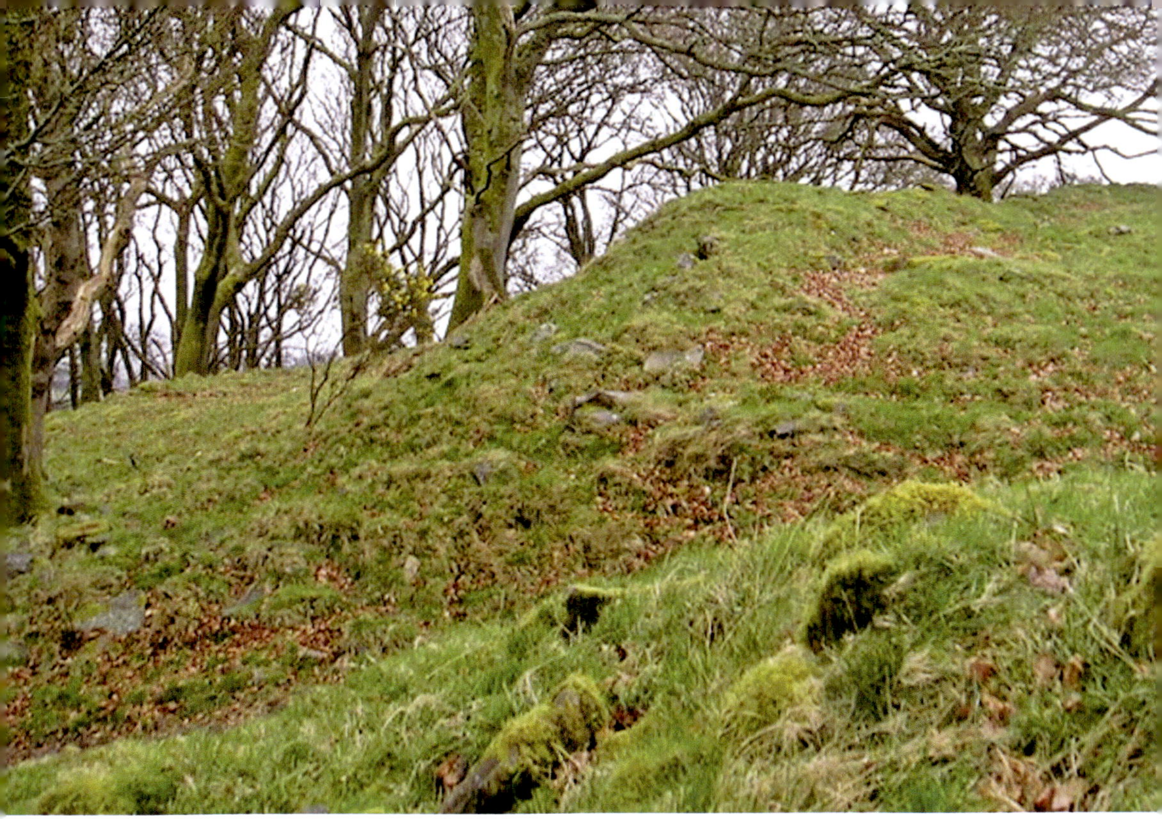

Entrance to Craig-Gwrtheyrn Camp. (Marion Phillips, CC BY-SA 2.0)

The remains of a single massive rampart climbing towards a flat-topped hill can be seen at Merlin's Hill Fort, Abergwili. Once it was a triangular hill fort enclosed by timber defences. One mile west of the village of Llanfihangel-ar-Arth are the remains of Craig-gwrtheyrn Camp, a well-preserved example of an Iron Age hill fort, enclosing an area of around 1.5 hectares. Its defences measure 520 feet north to south, and 410 feet east to west, and follow the contours of the hill. Only traces remain of the drystone rampart, originally 6.6 to 9.8 feet thick. There is an entrance along the south-west where two further banks create a barbican and the remains of a rare defensive feature exist, thirty sharp ended stones set on end.

When Roman forces arrived in Wales, they set about systematically destroying tribal symbols of power and wealth and removing all opposition. Archaeological evidence reveals many hill forts were destroyed by fire and their defenders butchered. In Carmarthenshire there is no evidence of such activity, suggesting the Roman arrival was a more peaceful and negotiated affair.

Until forts could be established, the Romans reinforced hill forts, using them to conduct military operations, develop trade, gather taxes and steer local tribes towards peaceful self-government. In time Roman fortifications dominated the landscape. First, they built large wooden fortifications, later replaced with stone forts. In Carmarthenshire three large forts were constructed around 75 CE along with several fortlets (small forts), and the remains of several marching camps still exist.

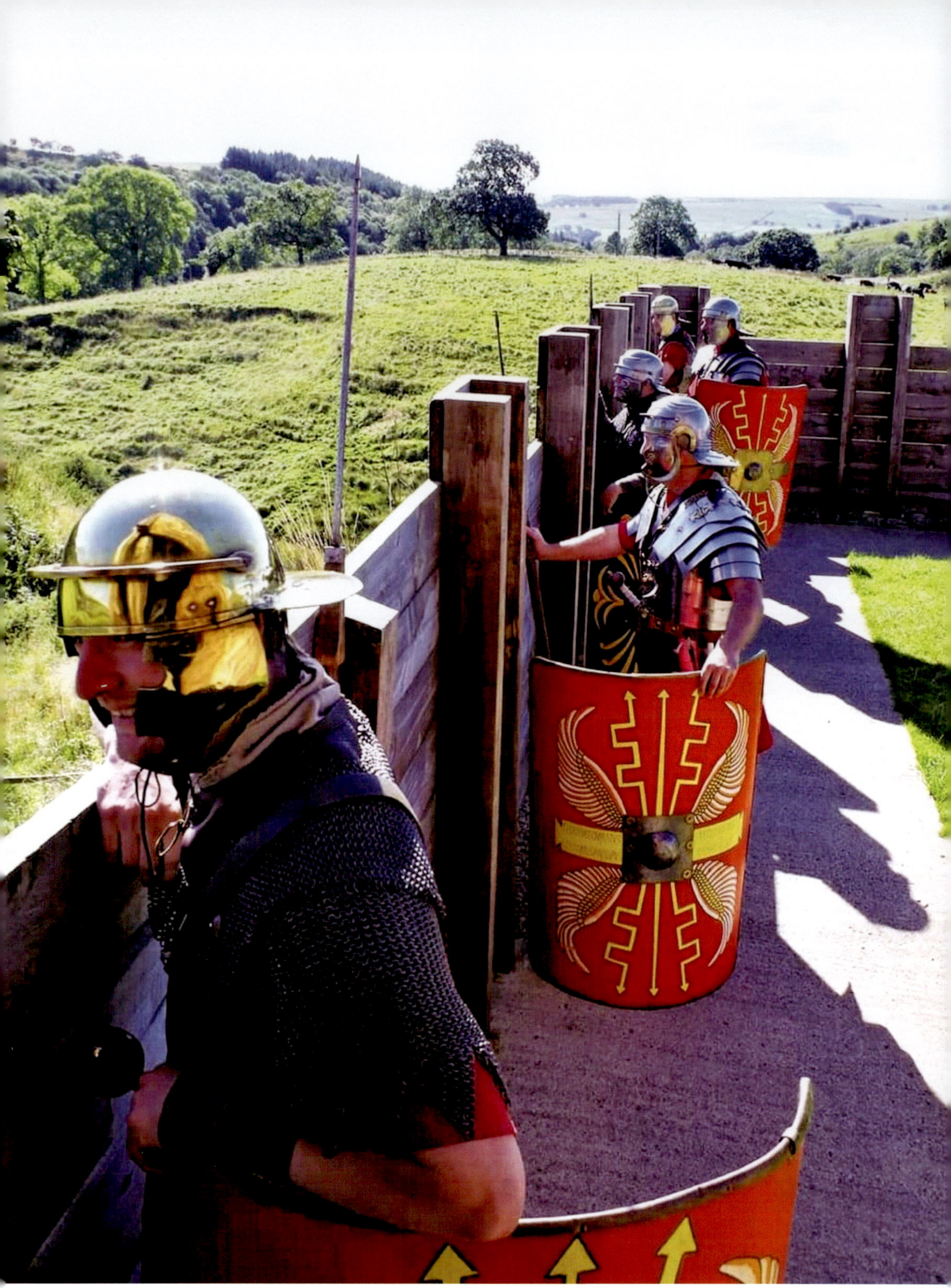

Roman re-enactors guarding a fort. (NS)

Roman seaborne forces operating out of Wales secured control of the western coast and estuaries. They built a Moridunum (Sea Fort) at Carmarthen, which became the administrative centre of the Romanised Demetae tribe. It was occupied until 120 CE and most of the fort and towns remains lie under the streets of modern Carmarthen. The only Roman remains visible above ground is the amphitheatre, the most westerly in the Roman Empire and one of seven remaining in Britain, and two surviving in Wales.

Nearby on the south side of Carmarthen, Castell Collen Roman Road, are the remains of Abererbwll Roman Fortlet, a square, earthwork plateau situated on a hilltop. Around 140 feet across, half is on the open hillside, the remainder in Crychan Forest. Remnants of a ditch can be seen in the forestry.

When the Romans seized the gold workings at Dolaucothi, near Pumsaint, Llanwrda, in 120 CE, they built Luentinum, a wooden fort defended by turf and clay banks with a double ditch. Luentinum can be found at the junction of several Roman roads running to Carmarthen and St Davids. It was later rebuilt in stone, then abandoned around 150 CE. Today the remains of the fort lie beneath the village of Pumsaint.

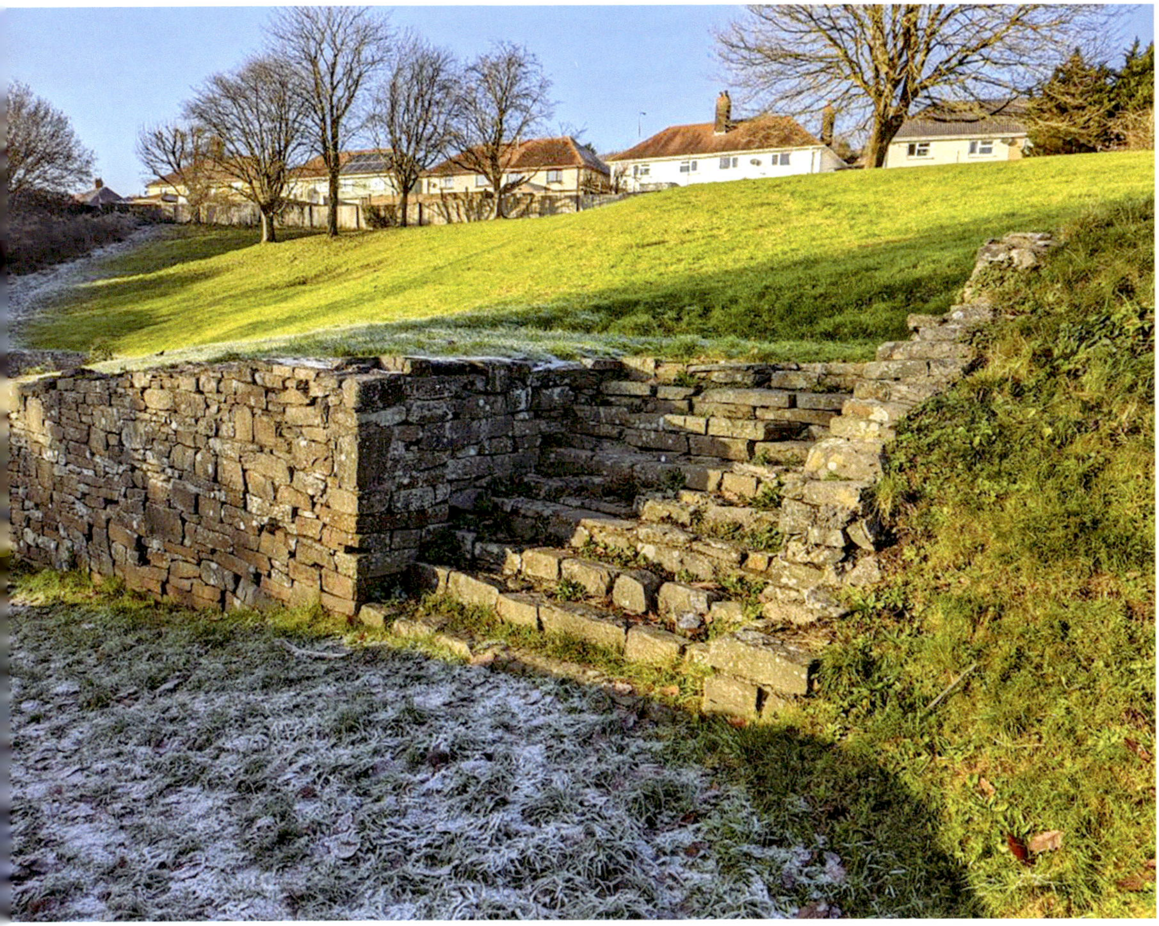

Amphitheatre – Carmarthen.

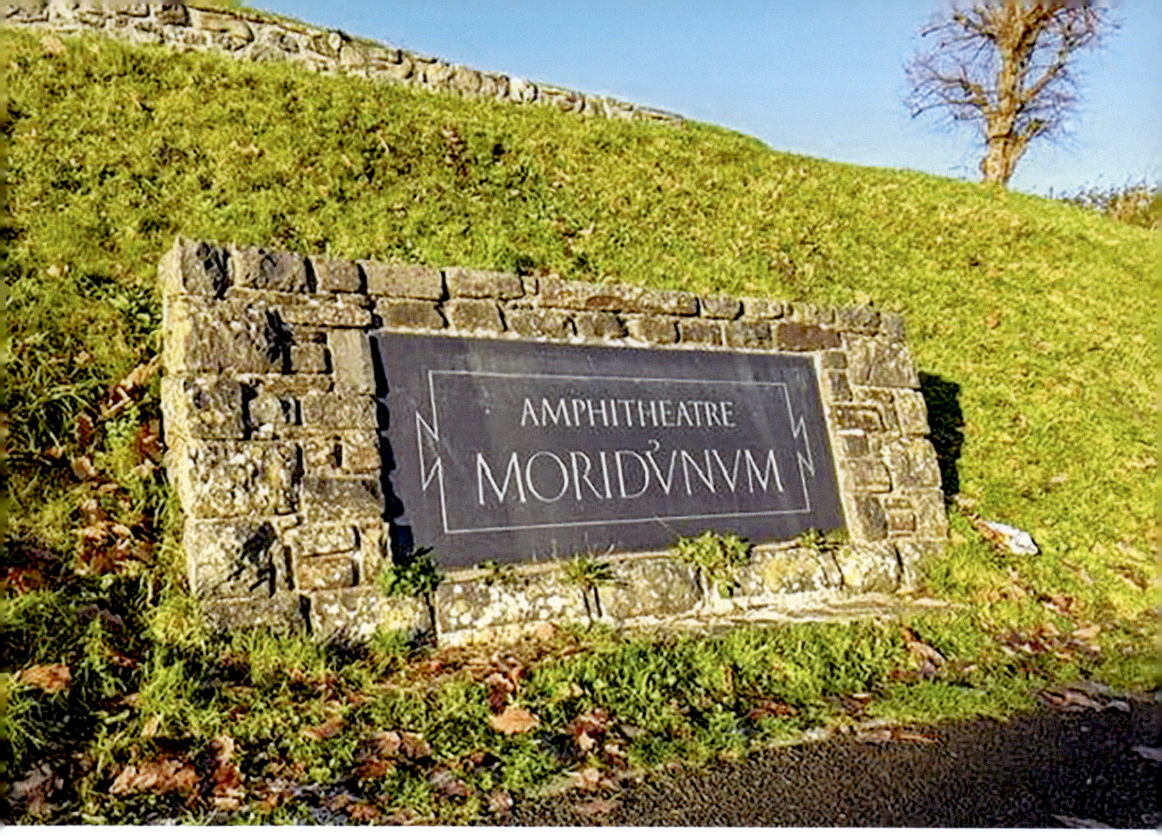

One of the roads from the Dolaucothi gold mines goes to Llandovery, where an auxiliary fort (Alabum) was built upon Llanfair Hill in 75 CE, as part of the Roman offensive into South Wales. Defended by a double-ditch and clay rampart, and later strengthened with a stone revetment wall, the site covered an area of 5.25 acres.

The medieval stone church of St Mary was built within the fort's earthworks and pieces of Roman tiles can be seen embedded in the church walls. A Scheduled Ancient Monument, the best-preserved section of the earthworks is the scarped banks along the western section.

The earthwork of a Roman fortlet, 270 feet square, with rounded corners, occupies a site midway between the Llandovery and Caerau forts. Now obscured by forestry, it once provided extensive views to the north-west. The forest also covers part of the earthwork, and the only evidence of an entrance is on the south-eastern side, although experts believe there were entrances in the centre of each side.

The remains of another Roman fortlet or signal station can be found south-west of Gallt yr Adar Fawr, overlooking the Afon Dulais. This one is rectangular with rounded corners and encloses an area measuring approximately 20 metres by 24 metres. Made of a bank and external ditch, the bank is up to 13 feet wide and stands approximately 1 foot above the ditch. The ditch varies in width, but some parts are up to 9 feet wide and 1 foot deep. Faint banks can be seen subdividing the south side into two rectangles.

At Y Pigwn, to the north of the Roman road between Brecon and Llandovery, are the Trecastle marching camps and fortlet, two large superimposed temporary marching camps. The larger camp covers 37 and a half acres and the smaller 25 acres. Nearby is a small square camp with rounded corners, each side measuring only 114 feet, and covering just over a quarter of an acre. At Mynydd Myddfai, half a mile west of Y-Pigwn on a spur between two tributary streams of the Afon Gwydderig and overlooking Hafod Fawr, are the remnants of a small fortlet covering an area of one third of an acre.

The earliest visible Roman military structure in Carmarthenshire is at Arosfa Gareg-Llwyd, Llanddeusant, the remains of a marching camp, a temporary base used by Roman legions. Here, the remaining earthworks are the typical playing card shape with round corners. Its length is aligned west, north-west to east, north-east; elongated slightly on the north, north-east side; and it measures 1,601 feet by 1,197 feet. The traceable earthworks consist of a bank between 14 and 18 feet wide and up to 2 feet high. With a shallow outer ditch measuring 5 feet wide and 6 inches deep. Its counterscarp bank, measuring 1 foot high and 11 feet wide, is also visible.

Pen-y- Castell, a temporary Roman camp from which Roman soldiers guarded the ford crossing the River Lliedi, is believed to have existed in the town of Llanelli, on an area bounded by buildings known as 'The Metropolitan'. Cartographical evidence suggests the existence in that location of a classic 'playing card' shape fort, which Victorian historian Arthur Mee (1888) attributes to being Roman. The site was built over in the late nineteenth century, but today a blue plaque on the wall of 'The Metropolitan' in John Street marks the north-west corner of the earthwork.

These formidable structures enabled Roman forces to command and control for centuries. When they left, many more centuries would pass before the next great fortifications were constructed and new overlords would come to pass.

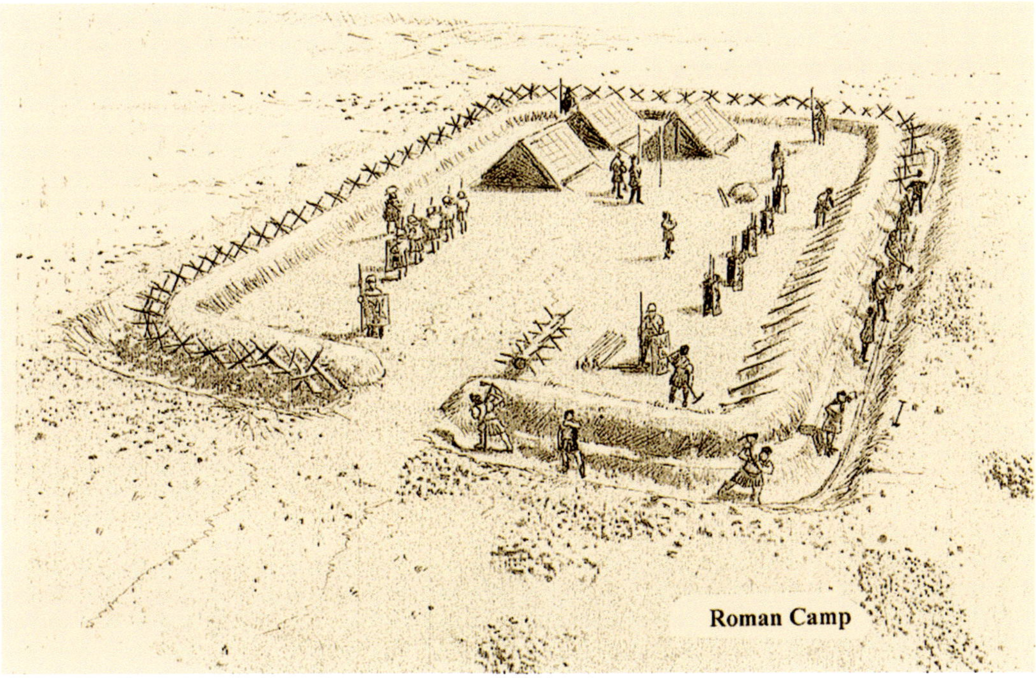

Artist's impression of Pen-Y-Castell. (JH)

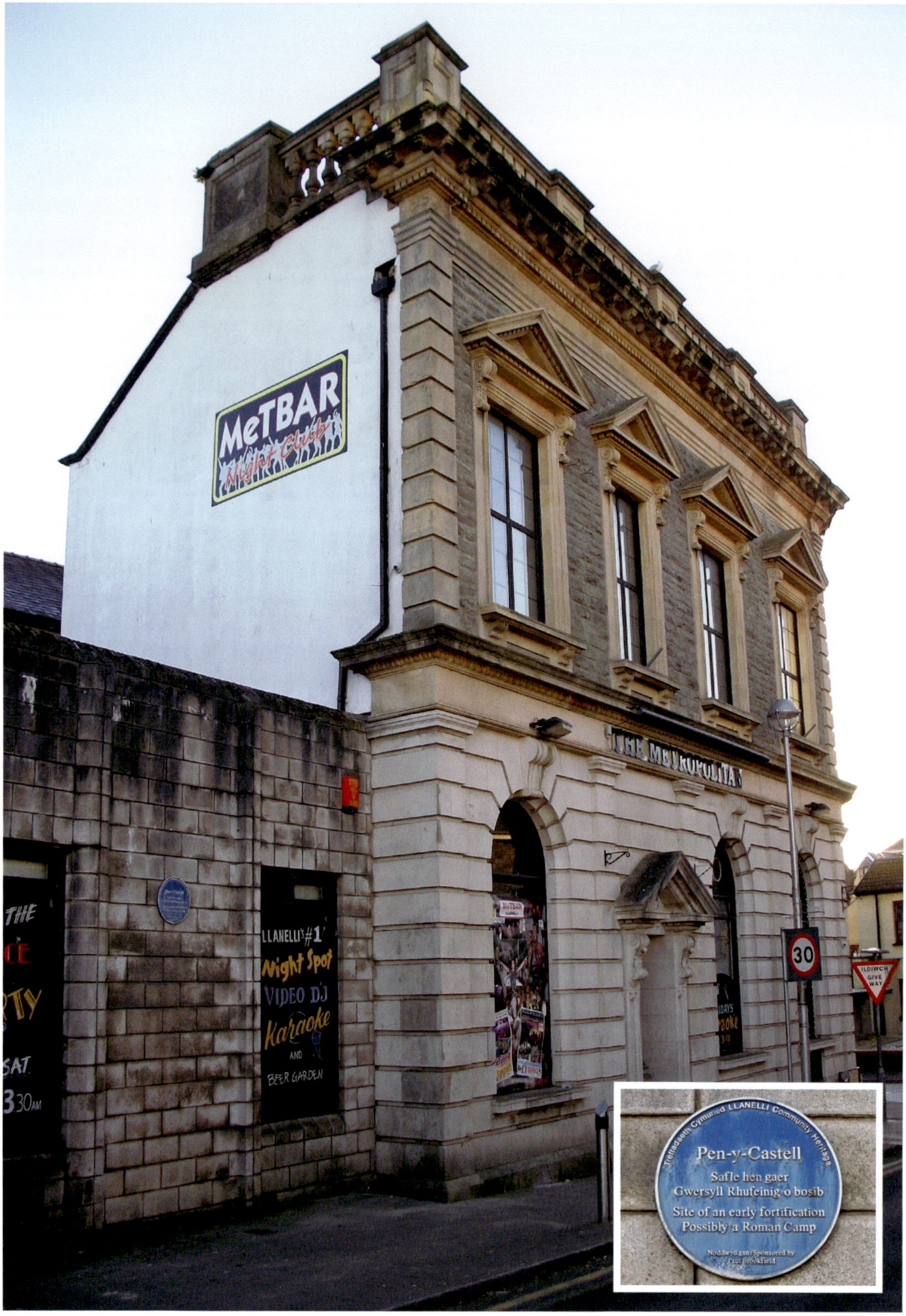

John Street, Llanelli.

3

Castles and Bunkers

The Welsh countryside is rich with the remains of stone castles built during the Middle Ages by Welsh princes to intimidate, subjugate, and dominate the population whilst warding off the advances of warring leaders. When the Norman and Edwardian forces arrived, they destroyed many Welsh-built castles, then rebuilt them to deter would be insurgents and repel future aggressors. The history of the castle builders is told and seen across Carmarthenshire, showing in the heritage of the castles that remain today.

The Normans were expert castle builders who, following their invasion in 1066, began a building programme to increase their control over the English and the Welsh. Their first castles were artificial hills, known as a motte, with a wooden tower on top and an enclosed defended area known as a bailey at its base, defended by a ditch with a bank on the inside and a palisade on top.

A typical Norman motte-and-bailey castle with earthwork defences. Llangadog Castle was constructed in the late 1100s by the Lord of Cardigan, Gilbert de Clare. Prince Maelgwn ap Rhys besieged the castle in 1203, but following its capture it lapsed into disuse. Further attacks came in 1208 and 1209, when the Prince of Deheubarth, Maelgwn ap Rhys finally demolished Llangadog Castle. While the remains of several motte-and-baileys exist, the best is at St Clears where, on the junction between the Taf and Cynin rivers, are the remains of an impressive motte and bailey that once carried a stone keep. The well-preserved remnants of the motte stand 26 feet high and across its top measures 65 feet by 32 feet. The large rectangular bailey extends 164 feet south of the motte.

Having established their rule, the Normans began replacing motte-and-baily structures with stone castles. They built Carmarthen Castle on an outcrop above the River Tywi in 1105. Today the castle is mostly ruins; most of the curtain wall has been rebuilt, and while other features are visible, the best-preserved remains are the castles gatehouse and south-west tower.

One of Wales most romantic castles is Carreg Cennen, near Llandeilo. Perched on top of a sheer cliff, this Welsh castle was built during the thirteenth century by Lord Rhys of

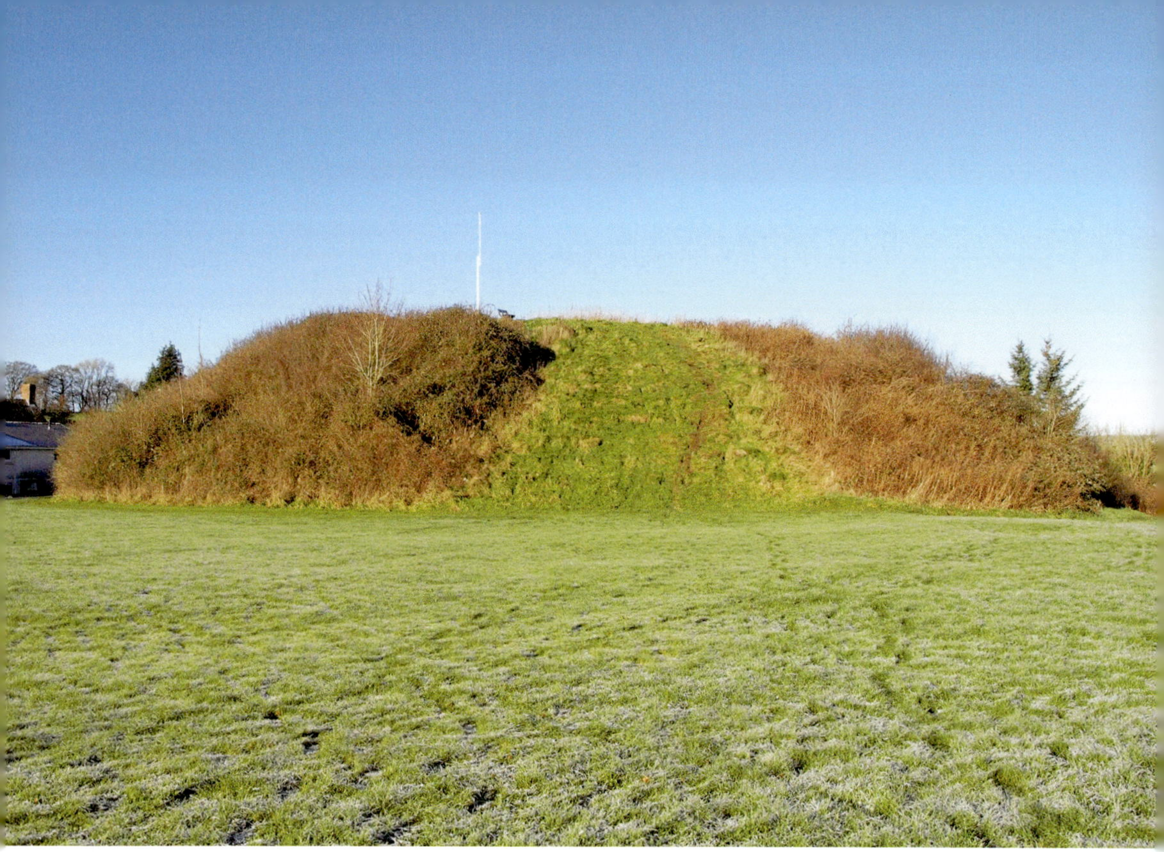

St Clear's Motte.

Deheubarth. The castle dominates the skyline and overlooks the River Cennen. It has had a long and eventful history, having been captured by Edward I of England and changing ownership several times. It is an atmospheric ruin today with many features, including a gatehouse, barbican, towers, and long sections of curtain wall.

Another castle with a commanding hilltop position is Dinefwr, which overlooks the Tywi valley. King Rhodri the Great built the first castle during the ninth century, and refortified by Lord Rhys, ruler of the kingdom of Deheubarth in 1160. During the early thirteenth century Llewelyn the Great dismantled and rebuilt it. These are the ruins seen today.

Dryslwyn in Llandeilo was once an important seat of the ancient kingdom of Deheubarth, and home to Dryslwyn Castle. One of the sons of Lord Rhys, Rhys Grug, built it in the 1220s and it remained in his family for several generations before the English king Edward I sent an army of 11,000 men to besiege it in 1287. The siege lasted from 24 August to 5 September. The English siege engines battered the castle walls and engineers dug tunnels under the foundations. Eventually the attackers collapsed a large section of the walls and captured the castle.

Kidwelly is Carmarthenshire's most striking and imposing medieval castle. It was built on the lowest bridge point on the River Gwendraeth after 1106 by Roger, Bishop of Salisbury, justiciar of England, as a Norman 'ringwork' castle made of wood and protected

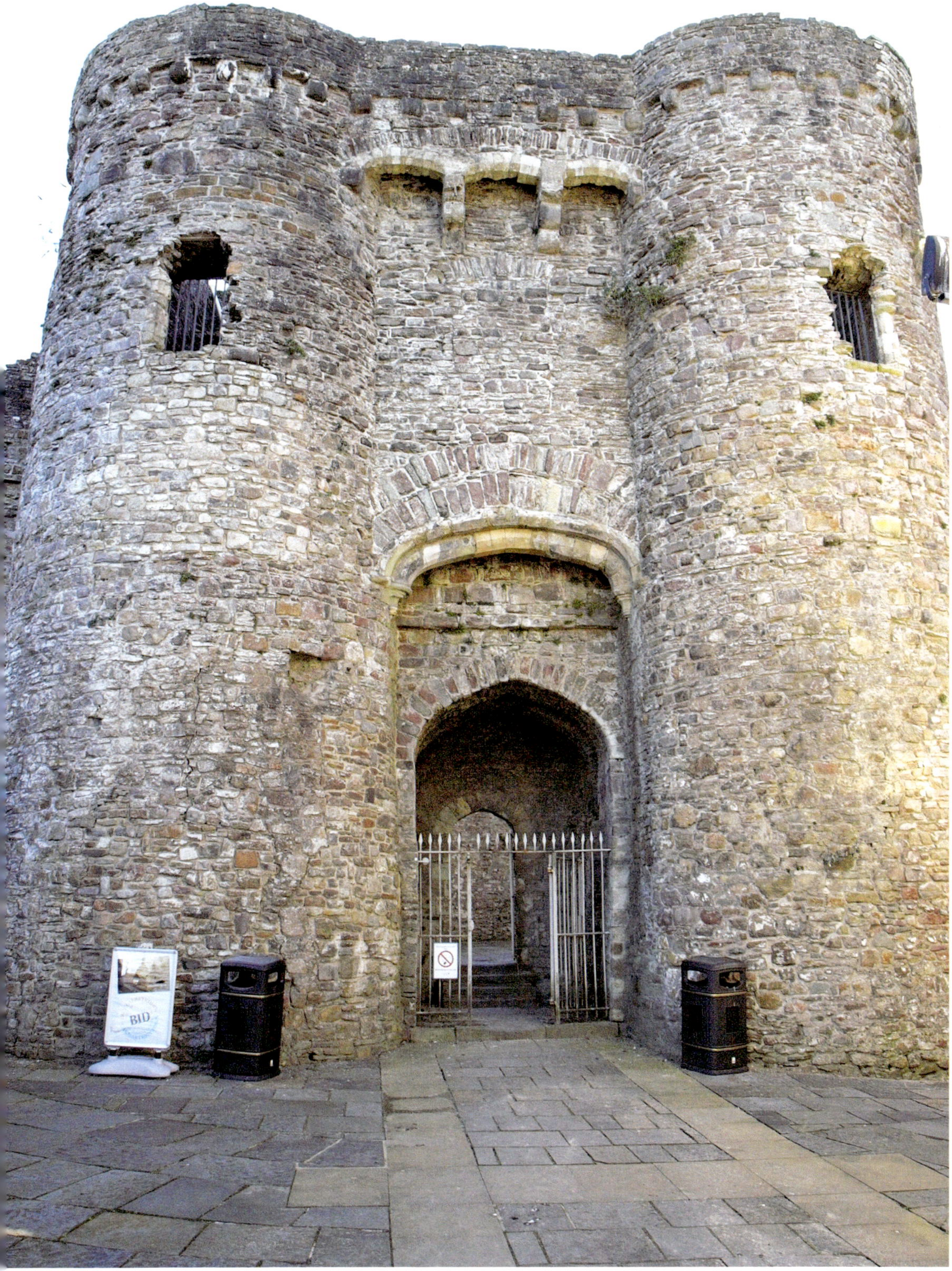

Gatehouse, Carmarthen Castle.

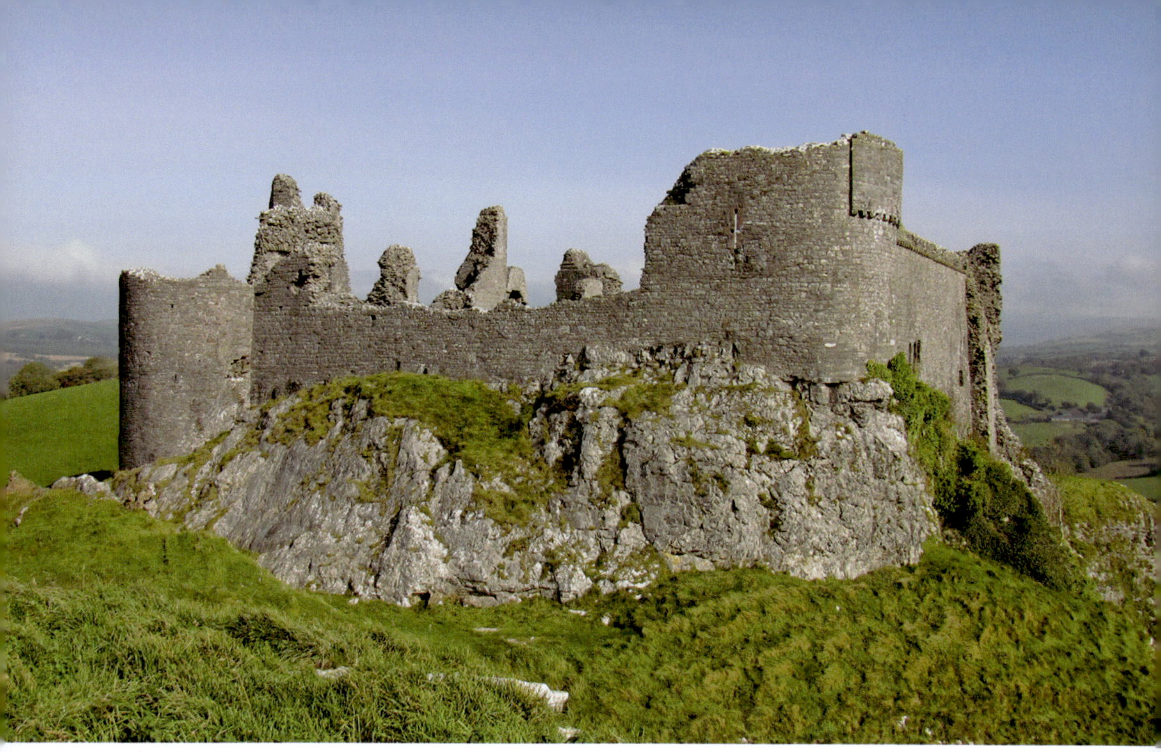

Carreg Cennen Castle. (Icebear917, CC BY-SA 4.0)

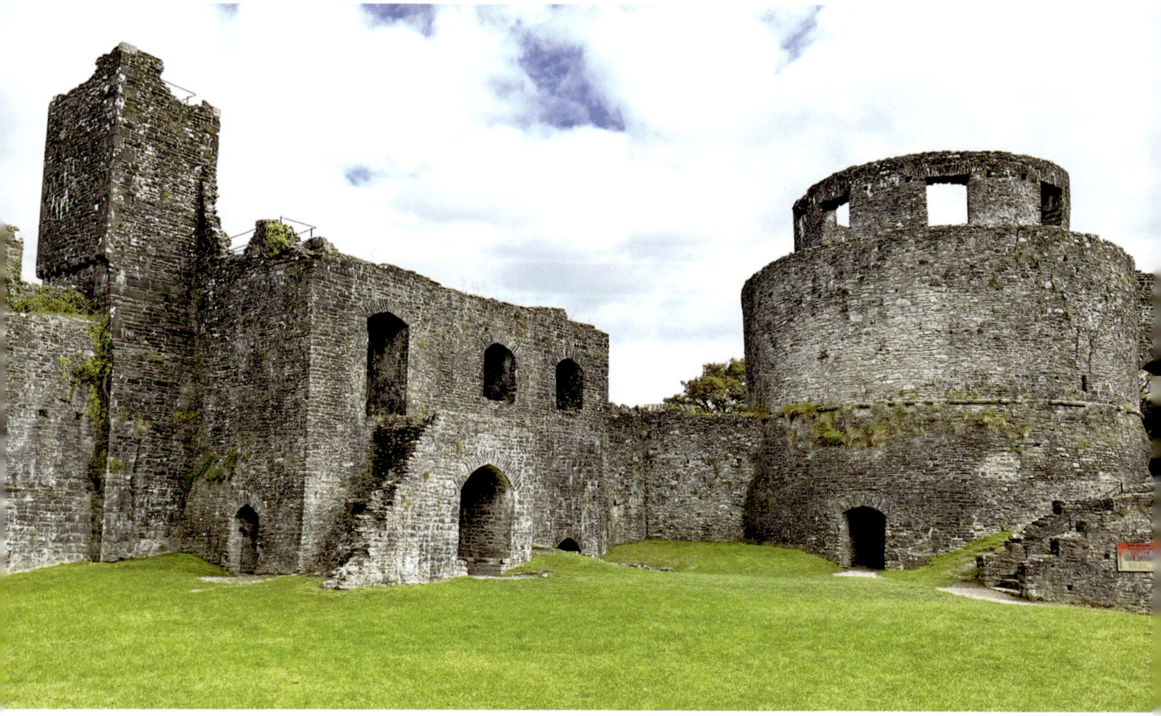

Ruins of Dinefwr Castle.

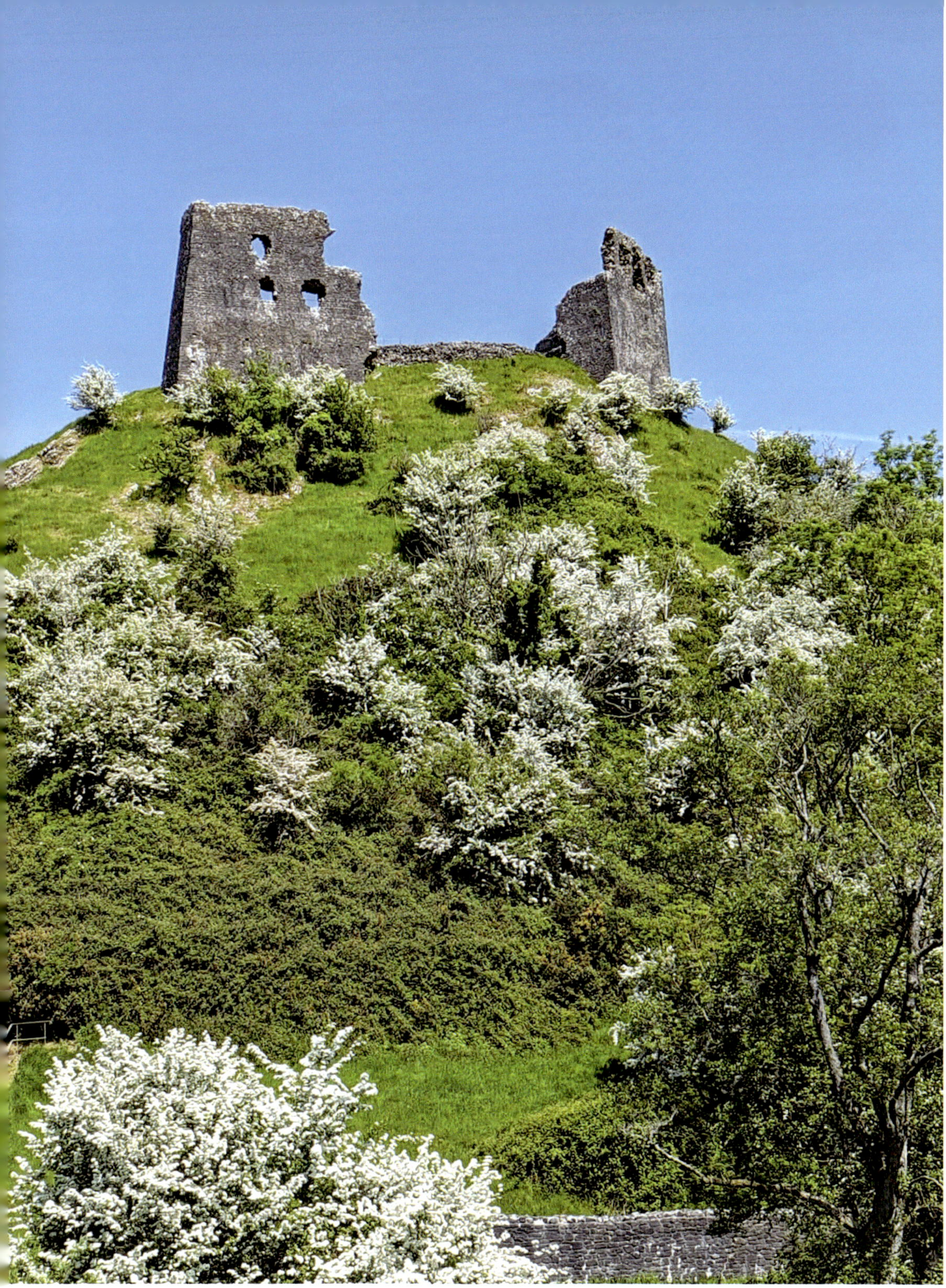
Dryslwyn Castle.

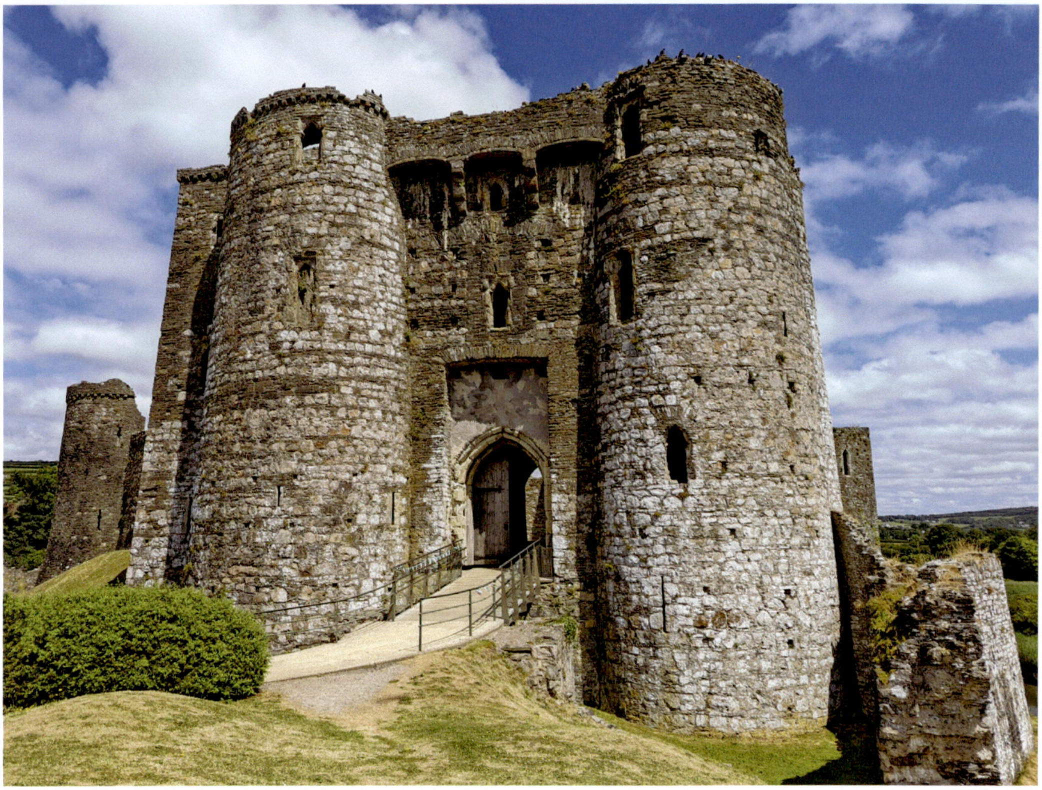

Kidwelly Castle.

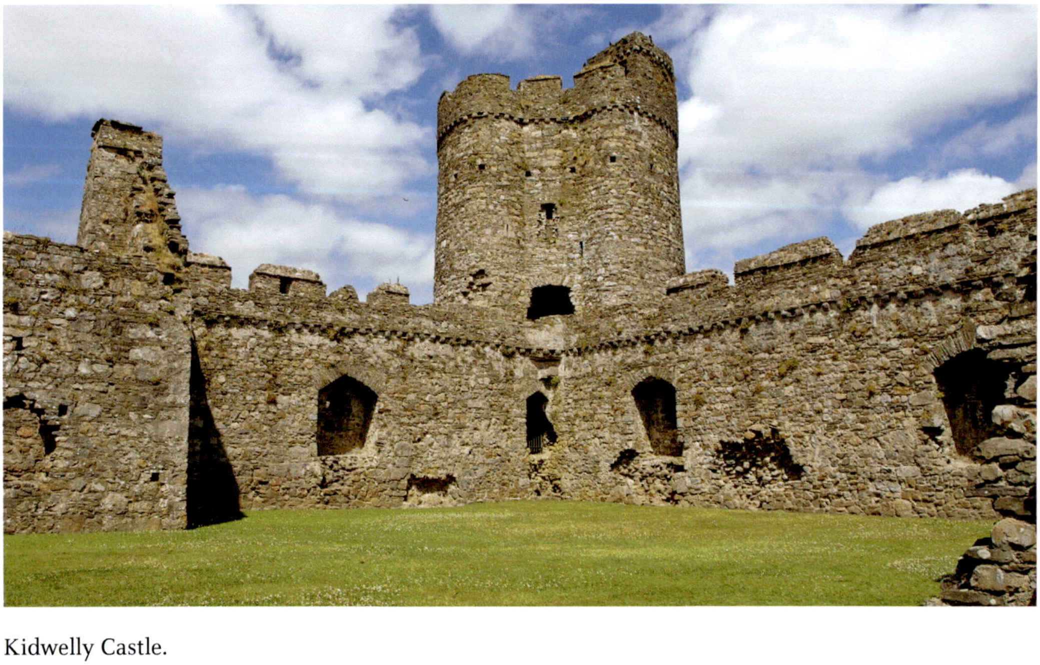

Kidwelly Castle.

only by an earthen bank and ditch. Welsh princes frequently attacked it, and Lord Rhys captured it in 1159.

The stone castle that stands today was built by a pair of 'Marcher' lords appointed by the king of England to guard the English–Welsh border during the 1280s. It was the object of many military engagements between Norman invaders and native princes with ownership and control changing numerous times. The full story is a book in its own right.

The castle's ruins are in good condition with most walls and turrets at their original height. Visitors can explore its sophisticated defence systems, including inner walls that follow the curve of its outer fortifications and ditch.

Laugharne Castle commands glorious views of the Taf estuary and is the county's most evocative fortification. Here, two giant medieval stone towers stand guard over the remains of a magnificent Tudor mansion. Created in the early twelfth century as a wooden fort, with earthwork fortification and a ringwork enclosure, some historians believe it is the famed Abercorran Castle captured by Lord Rhys in 1189. It was extended and modified several times and rebuilt in stone in the latter part of the twelfth century. By the thirteenth century it consisted of an inner court enclosed within a wall and ditch, defended by a large pair of circular stone towers. The inner fortifications were set inside an outer court with a huge

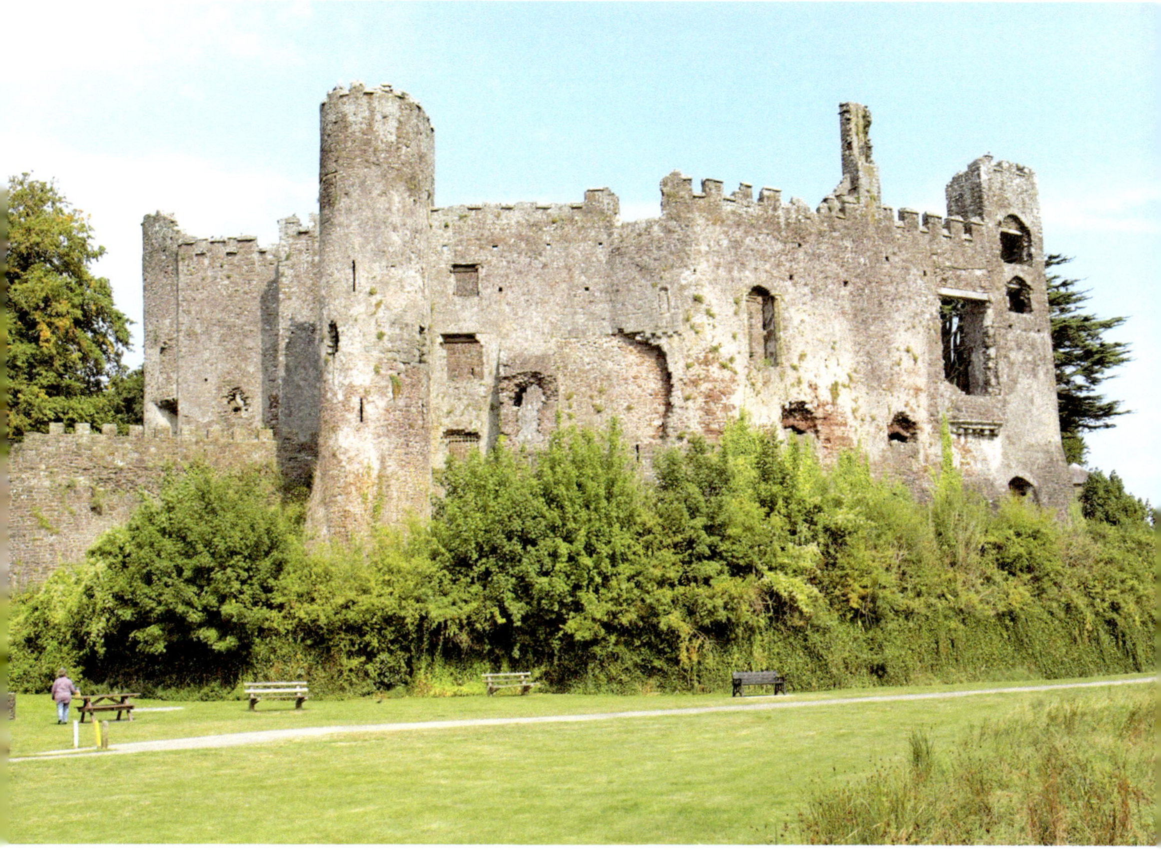

Laugharne Castle.

gatehouse to the north. An unusual feature at Laugharne Castle is the spectacular domed roof located in the north-west tower, which is one of the largest medieval domes in Wales.

Like Kidwelly, Laugharne Castle has endured centuries of conflict between Welsh and Anglo-Normans. It was saved from near ruin by high-flying Elizabethan courtier Sir John Perrot, who turned the dilapidated thirteenth-century castle into a residence fit for Elizabethan high society.

Despite being a comfortable home, it remained a fortified location and during the Civil War (1642–51) a Royalist force under Sir Charles Gerar captured it in 1644. A Parliamentarian force of 2,000 men under Major General Rowland held it to siege, and it was quickly retaken following a decisive night attack. The castle, severely damaged and partially demolished, was abandoned until the eighteenth century when a new mansion house was built in the sixteenth-century castle gardens.

Norman noble Richard Fitz Pons created the castle at Llandovery around 1100, and sculpted it on a natural hill to create a small bailey and a stone fortification. The castle was fiercely defended from several Welsh attacks, but captured by Rhys ap Gruffudd, the ruler of Deheubarth, in 1158. He rebuilt and improved its fortifications. After Rhys's death, his four sons clashed over his lands, and the castle changed hands five times in four years.

In 1277, on the orders of King Edward I, Baron John Giffard captured the castle to prevent it from falling back into Welsh hands. Giffard strengthened defences with a stone keep, curtain wall, and D-shaped tower. Llandovery was briefly taken by Llywelyn ap Gruffudd, during his revolt of 1282, and again by Rhys ap Maredudd, in 1287. The English

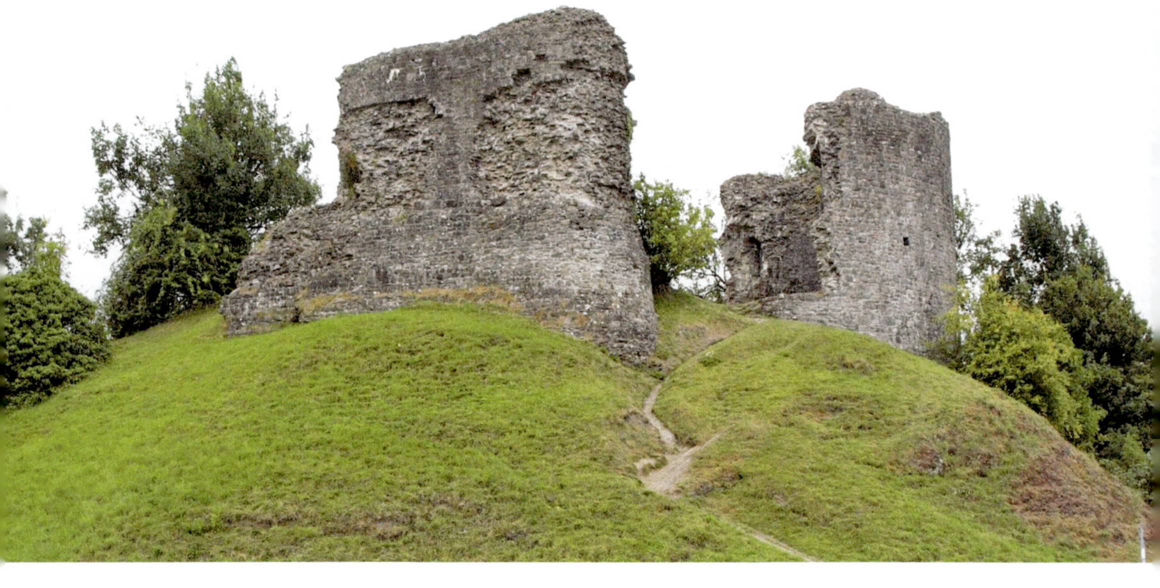

Llandovery Castle.

monarchy held it throughout its entire existence. All that stands now is the tower on the motte along with the remnants of the outer wall.

Llandovery Castle has a long and bloody history. The most gruesome event took place in 1401, when wealthy landowner Llewelyn ap Gruffudd Fychan was executed in the presence of King Henry IV as punishment for his support of Owain Glyndŵr, leader of the Welsh rebellion (1400–*c.* 1415).

The impressive, dramatic Llansteffan Castle stands on the headland overlooking the broad sandflats of the Tywi estuary, occupying the site of an Iron Age fort. Now a ruin, its twin three-storey gatehouse, flanked by two D-shaped towers, still looms large.

Lord Rhys and his brothers, princes of Deheubarth, captured the castle in 1146. By 1158 the area was under Norman control and Llansteffan Castle remained in English hands as home to Baron William de Camville and his descendants. The de Camvilles kept Llansteffan until 1338, building the stone fortress' ruins, which remain today. They temporarily lost

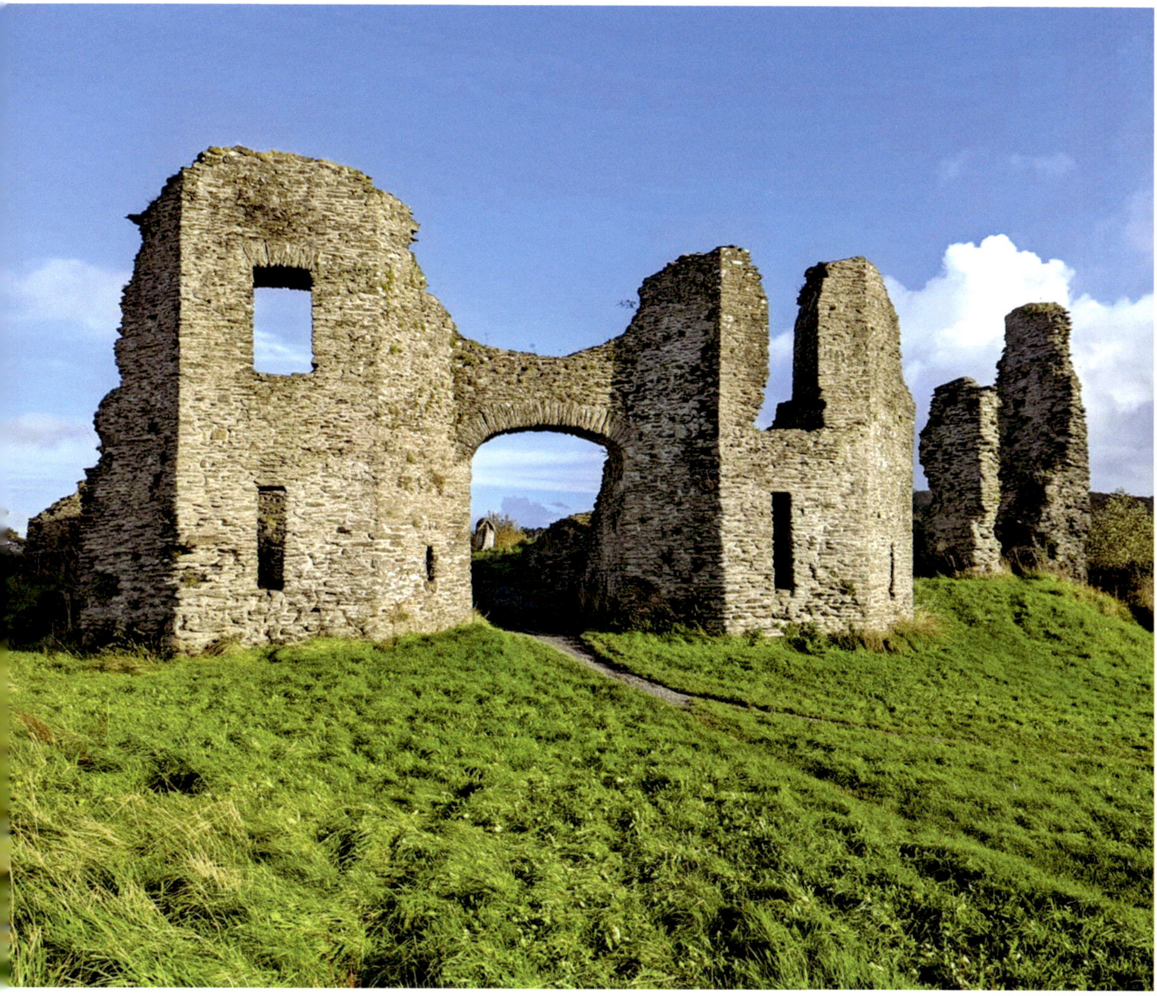

Newcastle Emlyn.

tenure during Welsh attacks in 1189, 1215 and 1257, but recaptured it. When the castles military importance declined, Llansteffan passed into obscurity.

The castle at Newcastle Emlyn occupies the tip of a steep-sided spur set within a great bend of the Teifi. The remains of its stone walls and fourteenth-century gatehouse are impressive, located in a walled inner court surrounded by earthwork defences. Meredith ap Rhys Gryg, Lord of Dynevor, constructed a new earthwork and timber castle at Emlyn in 1240 to administer the district of Emlyn Uwch Cych. He later rebuilt it in stone, although he intended it as an administrative, rather than a military, stronghold. Meredith's descendants supported the English during the Wars of Welsh Independence but later joined the rebellion of Rhys ap Maredud. It later saw action during both the rebellion of Owain Glyndŵr and the Civil War, when an English army, under Sir Thomas Carew, caused considerable damage to the castle and in the decades that followed it fell to ruin.

The castle became a royal fortress and was extensively modified and extended during the reigns of King Edward I and Edward II, who added a great hall in 1312. Edward III made further amendments. Welsh military leader Sir Rhys ap Thomas made the last major improvements. He converted the castle into a mansion around 1500 installing impressive Tudor style windows in the gatehouse.

The fragments of the county's most prolific defences are now as scarce as their predecessors, the stone castles. They were magnificent and built in the 1940s to repel and delay an invading force at a time when Britain's landscape was littered with fortified structures and defences. When they had served their purpose, many were demolished and have since become derelict or exist in remote locations, relicts of another era.

Following the fall of France in June 1940, Germany's Führer and Supreme Commander, Adolf Hitler, made it clear to the British government that rejecting the peace settlement he offered would result in his forces and the Axis powers destroying Britain and its empire. When his peace proposal was rejected, he activated Operation *Sea Lion*, the invasion of Britain. The invasion was to be seaborne, and he needed Germany to take control of the air first. To accomplish this, he had to destroy the Royal Air Force's capability, pilots, planes, airfields, and factories.

Aerial attacks on naval and commercial ports, military locations, munitions dumps, factories and other strategically important locations across the UK were to precede the assault. Fear of invasion gripped the nation, causing the government to authorise the construction of a series of defensive 'Stop Lines' and coastal defences. 'Stop Lines' were designed to stop a German advance long enough for the mobilisation of a reserve force capable of cutting supply lines and reinforcements. They also protected military and civilian targets, factories, and transport hubs. Their structure incorporated natural features, steep slopes, and rivers, a network of static defences, which included anti-tank ditches, anti-tank obstacles, called 'Dragons Teeth,' roadblocks, mine fields that have now been cleared, and numerous pillboxes. The latter were small fortified structures used to house anti-infantry and anti-tank weapons. Natural and manufactured features were reinforced and protected with gun emplacements, and rail, water, and land bridges rigged with explosives.

One of Carmarthenshire's more unusual gun emplacements exists at Cynwyl Elfed, part of the Carmarthen Stop Line: two houses fitted with machine gun loopholes. One also functioned as a roadblock with a steel cable stretched across the road, joined to a pair of rails embedded in the wall of the cottage.

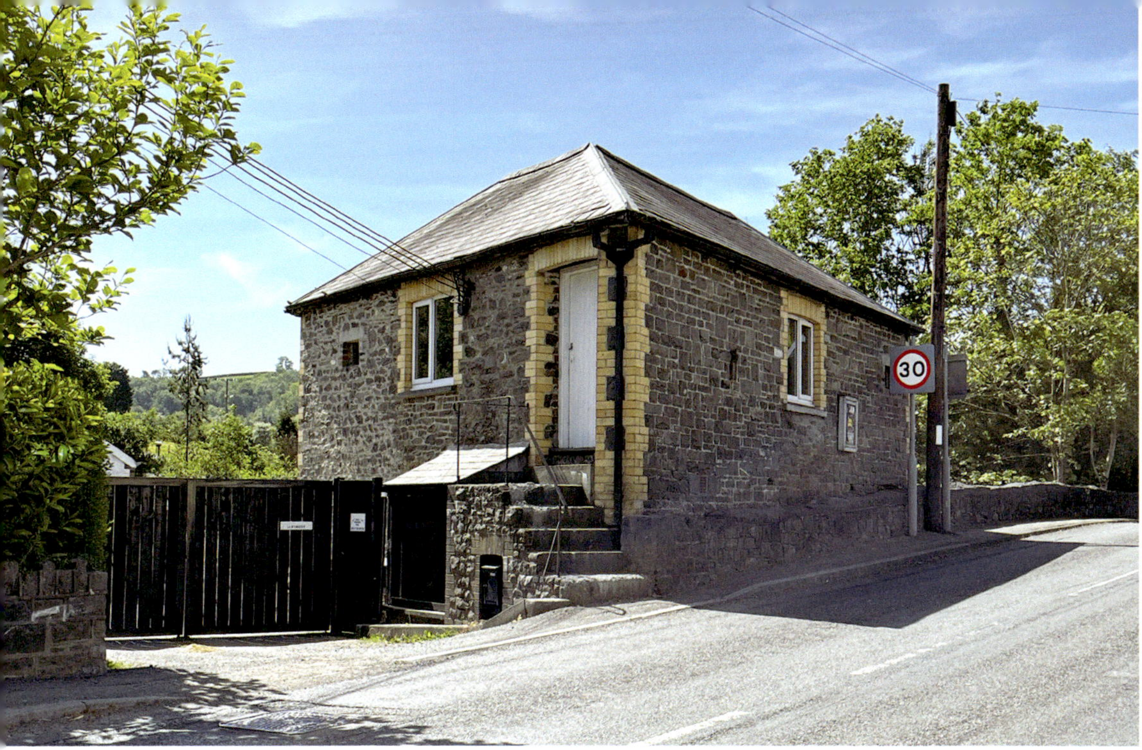

Defended building, Cynwyl Elfed.

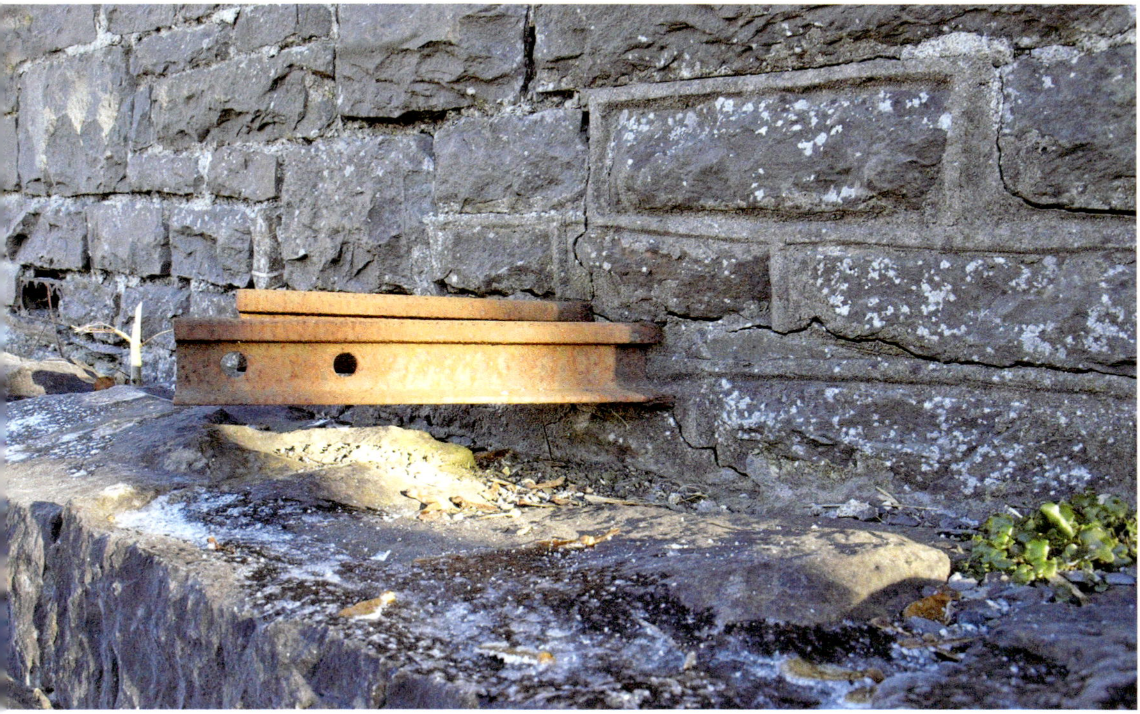

Defended building, Cynwyl Elfed.

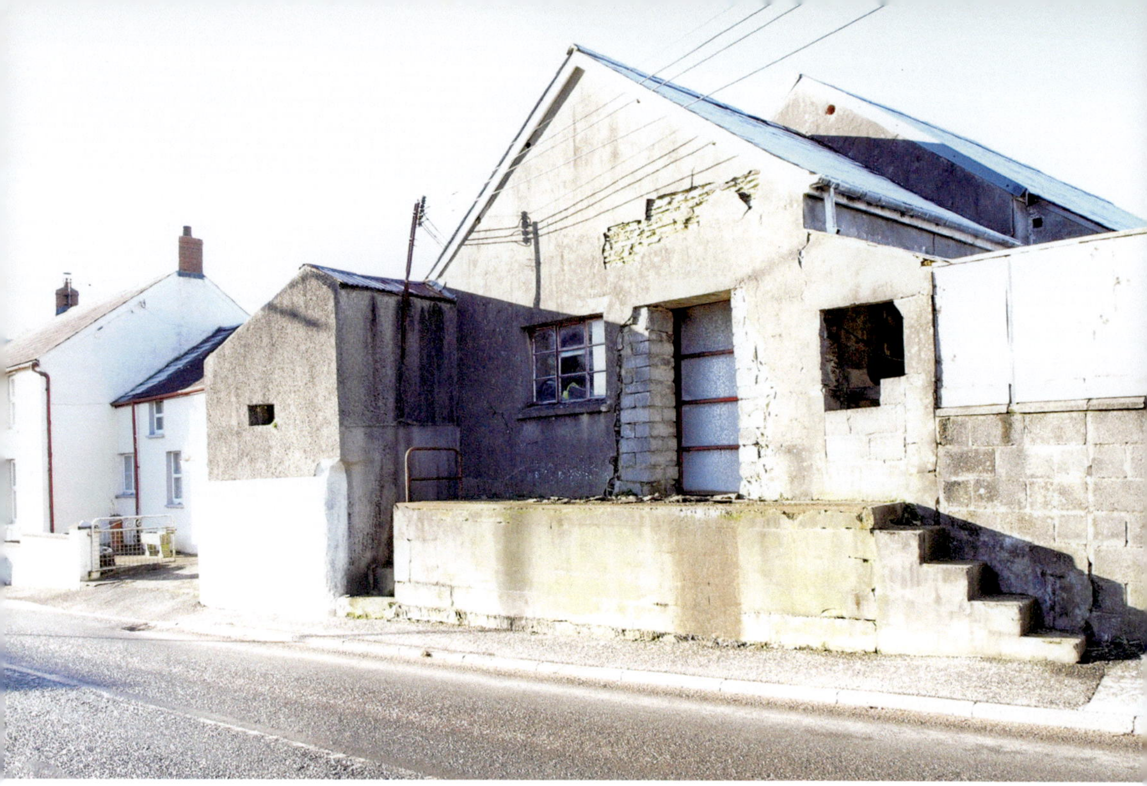

Defended building, Cynwyl Elfed.

Batteries of anti-aircraft guns and barrage balloons were deployed. These were to prevent low level strafing and bombing. Citizens were provided with personal and communal air-raid shelters.

In Carmarthenshire, the main line of anti-invasion defence was the Carmarthen 'Stop Line', which ran south to north along the River Towy and the Afon Duad, from the mouth of the Afon Tywi to Carmarthen, then to Cynwyl Elfed, Rhos, Henllan and Llangeler. From this point it continued north to Llangrannog and Pembrey.

Carmarthenshire's coastline was also reinforced with hardened field defences and while most installations no longer exist, many do and can be seen today. These include the remains of barbed wire entanglements, anti-tank vertical rails, anti-tank ditches, anti-tank walls, gun emplacements, various pillbox types, battery observation posts and many other military structures. For a comprehensive list of these defences and sites see the online Defence of Britain Archive.

In 1947, political and military tautness existed between the democratic west and communist nations in eastern Europe and Asia. This new 'Cold War' heralded a series of conflicts and international crises that increased tension, raised suspicions, and fuelled paranoia that nuclear war was imminent.

Britain's pre-emptive response was to build hundreds of secret underground bunkers that performed a variety of functions protecting key military, political and other influential figures in the event of a nuclear attack. The remains of these defences are by their very nature less visible and even less accessible.

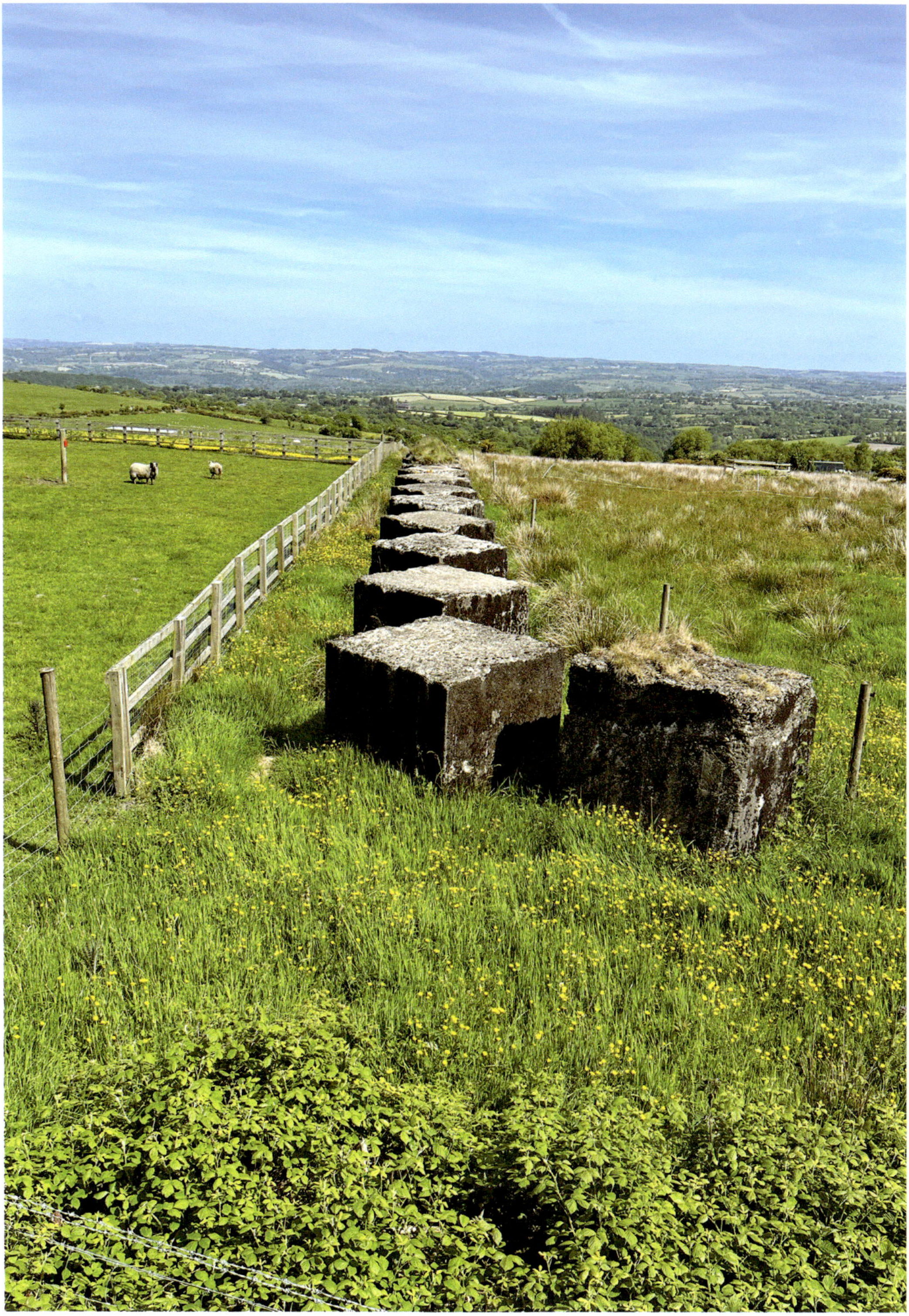

Anti-tank obstacles, Rhos.

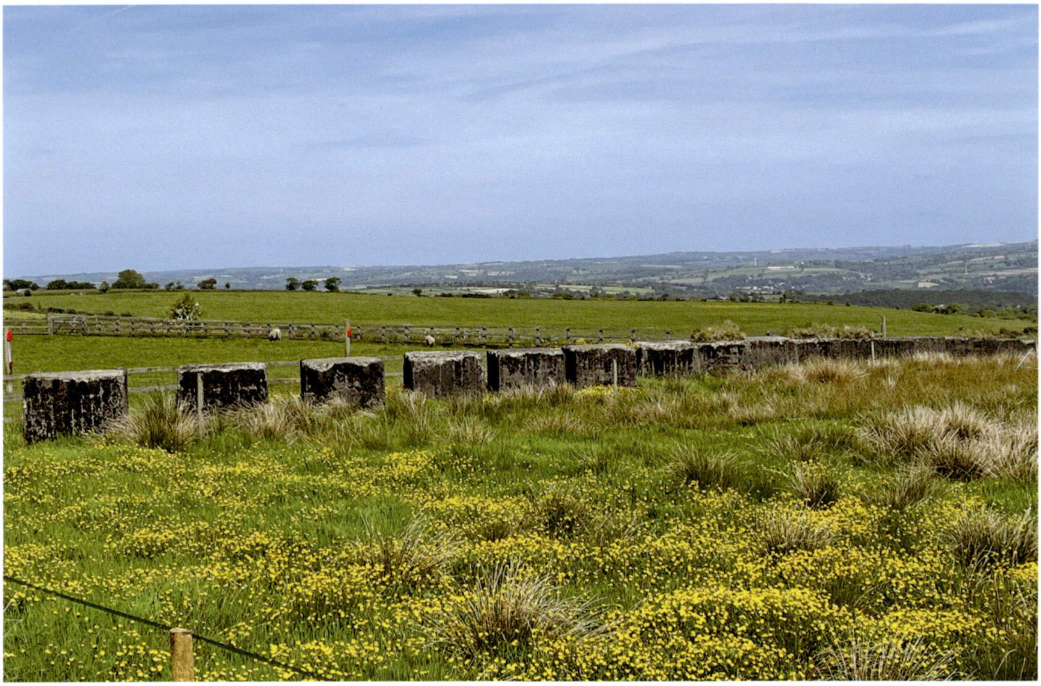

Anti-tank obstacles, Rhos.

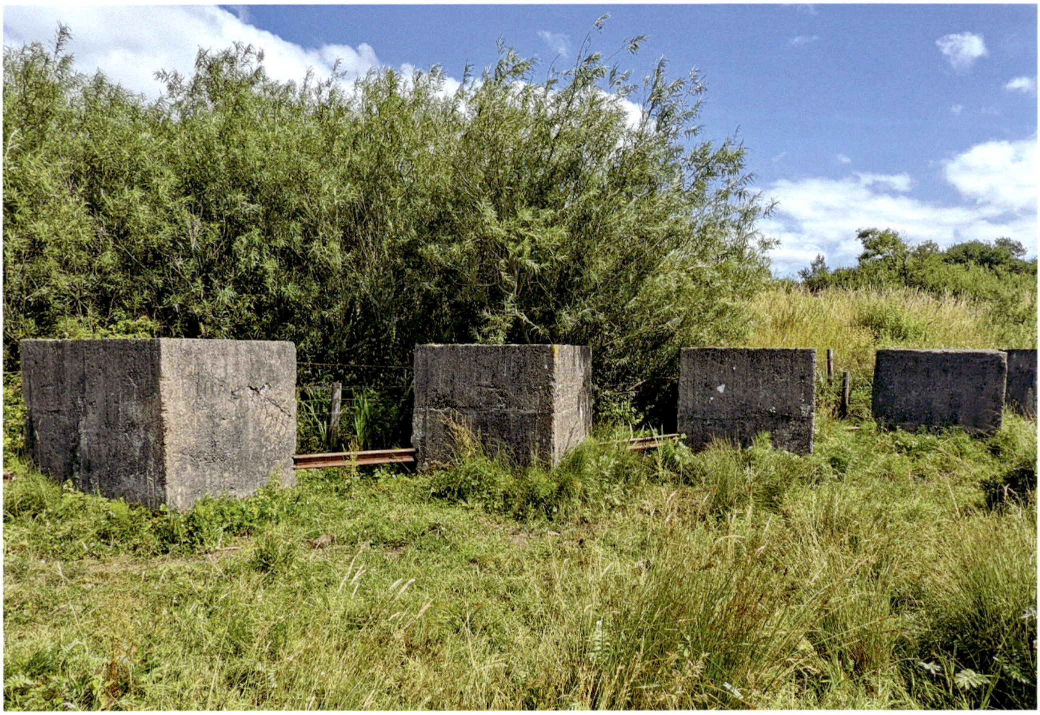

Anti-tank obstacles, Pembrey.

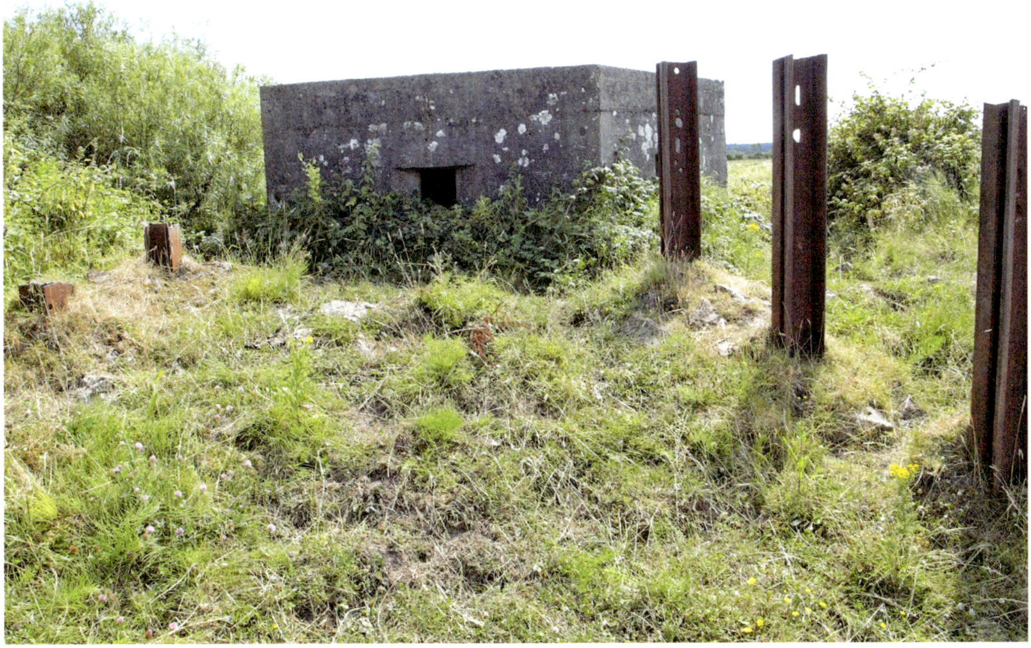

Anti-tank railings, Pembrey.

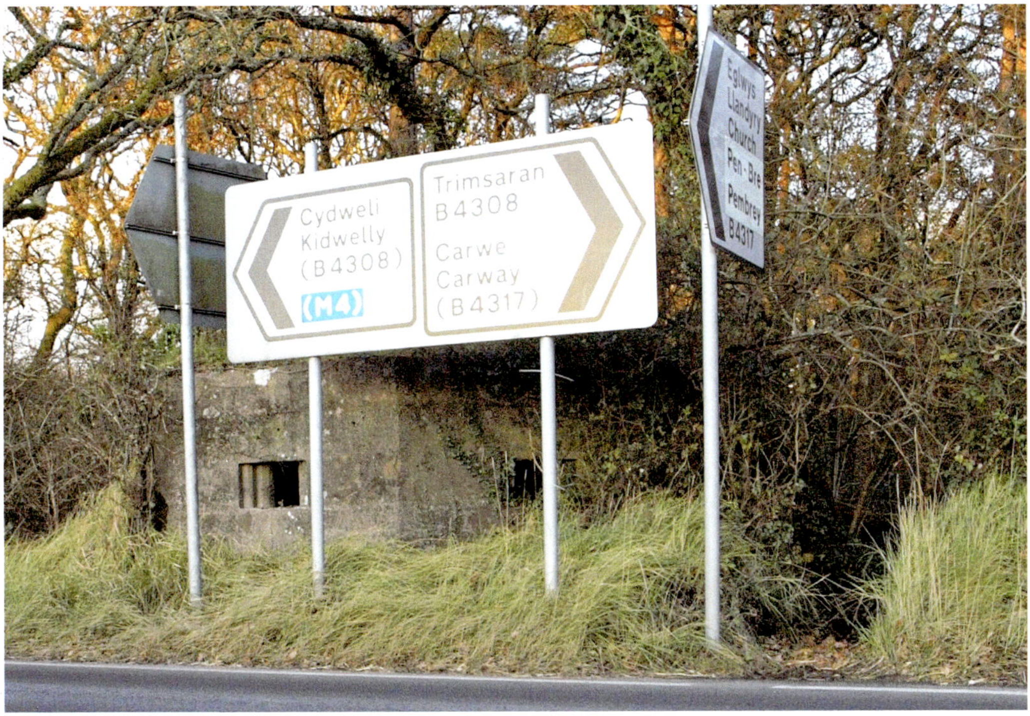

Pillbox, Trimsaran.

The most common bunkers (1,560) were monitoring posts and staffed by members of the Royal Observer Corp (ROC), a civil defence organisation. Small, three-person bunkers of uniform design, grouped in clusters of two to five posts, approximately 8 miles apart with one acting as the primary post. Their key function was to screen the effects of bomb bursts and radiation levels. Readings from several posts taken together could precisely locate where a nuclear weapon had hit. Half of the monitoring posts have been since demolished, and today most that survive are derelict.

The remains of eleven ROC monitoring posts exist at Carmarthen, Convill Dryslwyn, Pencader, Kidwelly, Laugharne, Llandysul, Llanboidy, Newcastle Emlyn, Newquay, and Pembrey Airfield. Here, the original surface features remain intact, and while nine are locked, at the time of writing Dryslwyn and Llandysul remain open.

Local monitoring posts reported to a local ROC Group Headquarters, and the remains of the Carmarthenshire Group Headquarters exist at the rear of the Army Reserve Centre, Picton Barracks, Picton Terrace, Carmarthen. The building, clad in corrugated metal sheeting and painted dark green, is all that remains of the former Cold War site.

The county's only other Cold War bunker is beneath the staff car park of the County Council's headquarters. The Carmarthen County Council Control Bunker, built during the 1980s, housed the county's 'Emergency Council Control (EGC)' and was intended to provide government continuity in the aftermath of a nuclear attack. The only evidence of the EGC's existence is a large oblong metal grid in the centre of the car park.

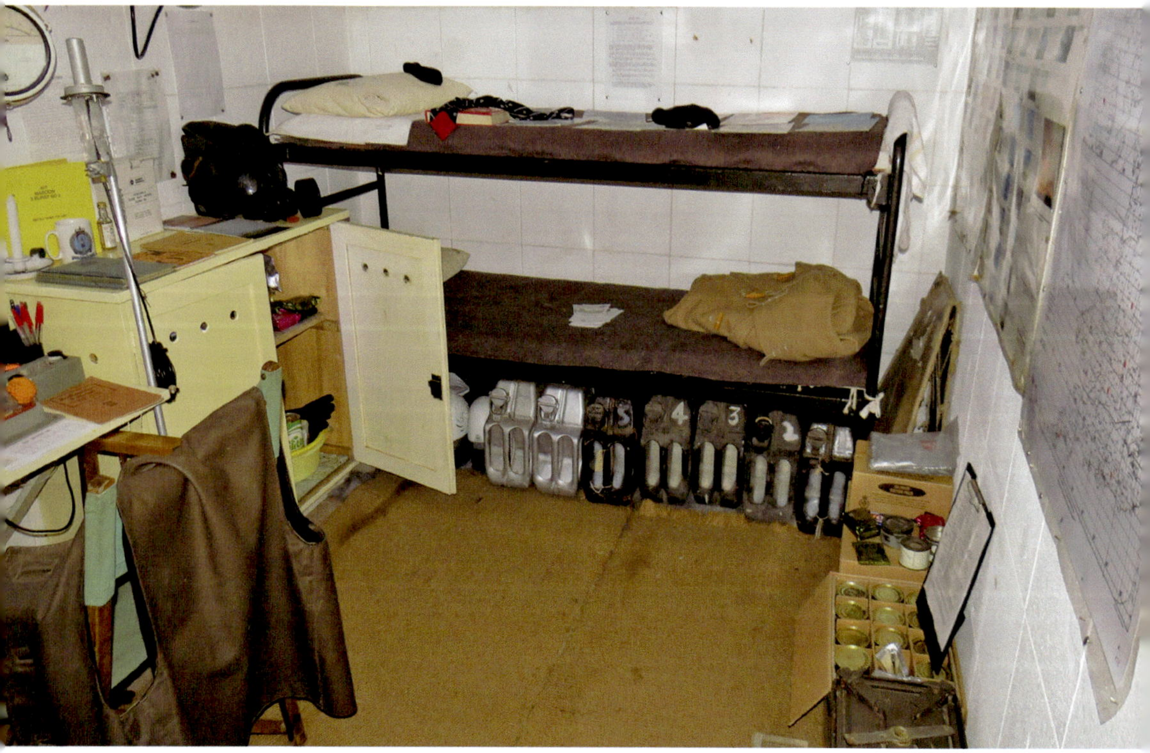

Inside an ROC post.

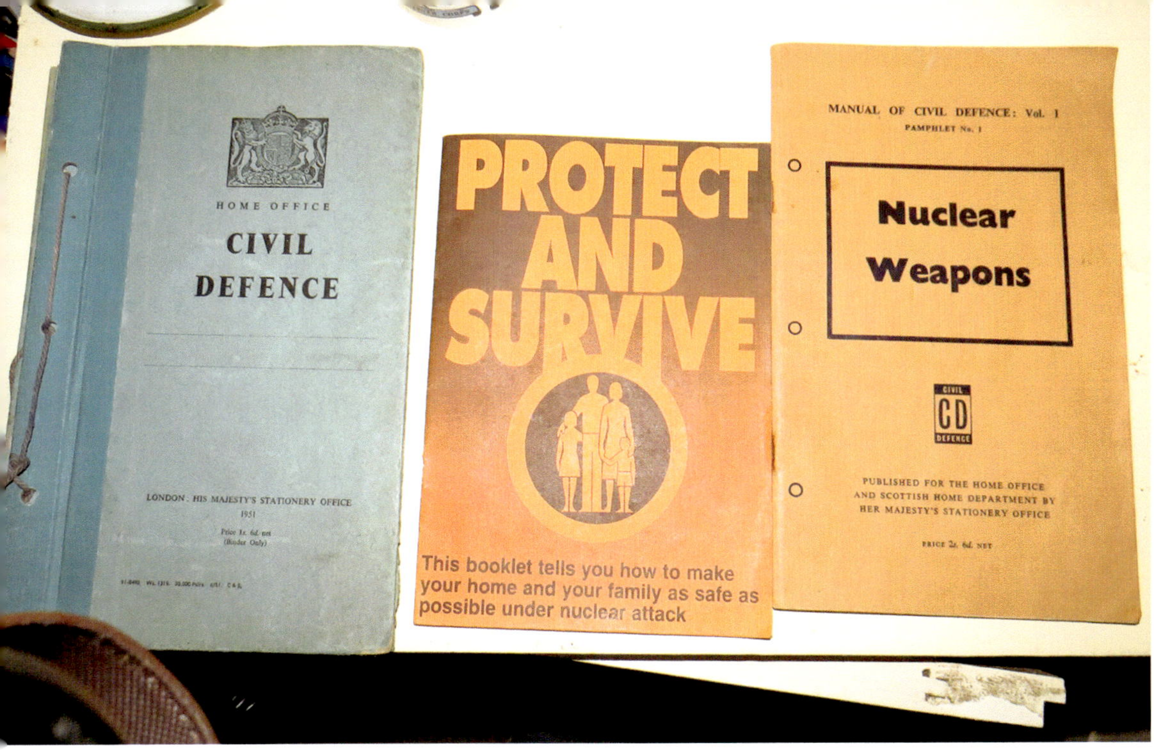

Inside an ROC post.

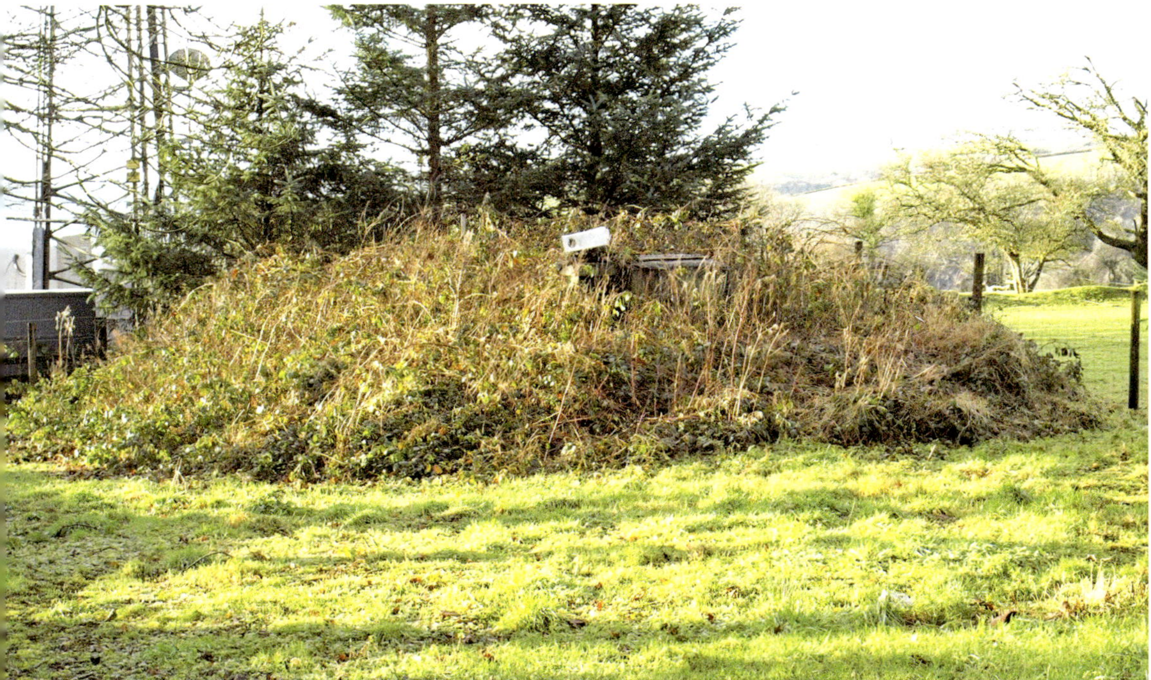

ROC post, Pencader.

4

Riots and Revolts

Over the centuries Carmarthenshire has witnessed and played host to many rebellions, riots, and revolts. These include the Great Revolt of 1136 against incoming English, Norman, and Flemish forces; the Glyndŵr Rising of 1400, a fifteen-year rebellion against the Kingdom of England; and the Welsh Rebellion against the English Civil War (1642–1651). This chapter presents three contemporary accounts of insurrection and resistance against authority.

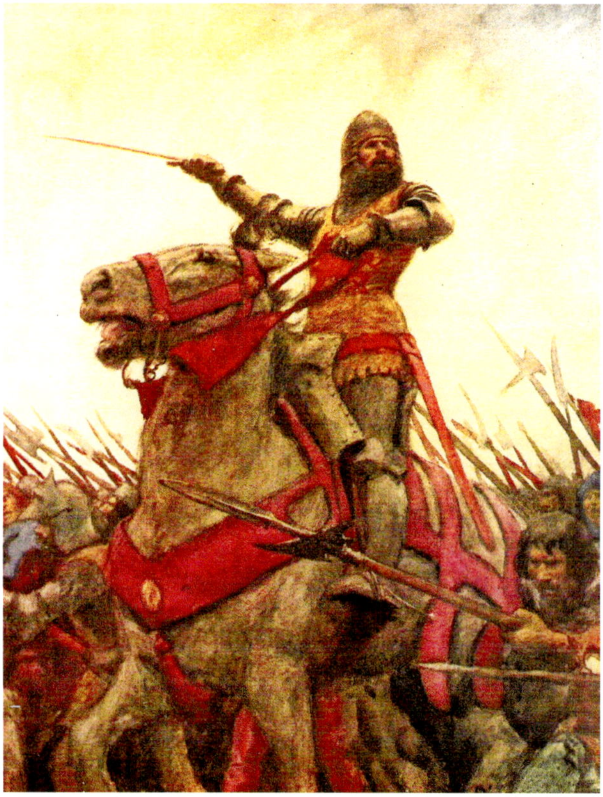

Glyndŵr Rising, Arthur Cadwgan Michael (1881–1965).

During the eighteenth and early nineteenth centuries, there were no police forces in West Wales. In times of civil unrest, special constables were sworn in, and regular soldiers and volunteers from the local militia and yeomanry's were deployed to keep the peace. In 1839, the Rural Constabulary Act allowed county areas to establish police forces. The counties of West Wales thought this was too expensive and continued their policy of relying on special constables and soldiers to quell uprisings.

The Carmarthen Cheese Riot of 1818 is one of the counties lesser-known riots. Vital to the diets of Welsh people, cheese was a source of protein and calcium and an important substitute for meat.

When on 25 September 1818 local people learnt merchants were loading cheeses onto ships for export, rather than keeping them for the people of Carmarthenshire, it infuriated them, and they gathered en masse at the quay. When attempts by merchants, the mayor, and magistrates to disperse the crowd failed, they began removing the cheese from the ships and returning it to the warehouses.

Two days later a ringing bell alerted residents that merchants were loading cheeses onto a ship. Furious residents descended upon the quay and stormed the ship, ransacking it and smashing its cargo. The mayor immediately summoned two troops of the Carmarthen Yeomanry, under the command of Captain's Jones and Howell, along with a platoon of the Royal Carmarthen Rifle Regiment (Militia) led by Captain Harding.

Having seized the cheese and returned it to the warehouse, the rioters waited to see what the merchants and authorities would do next. Keen to avoid further rioting, the merchants

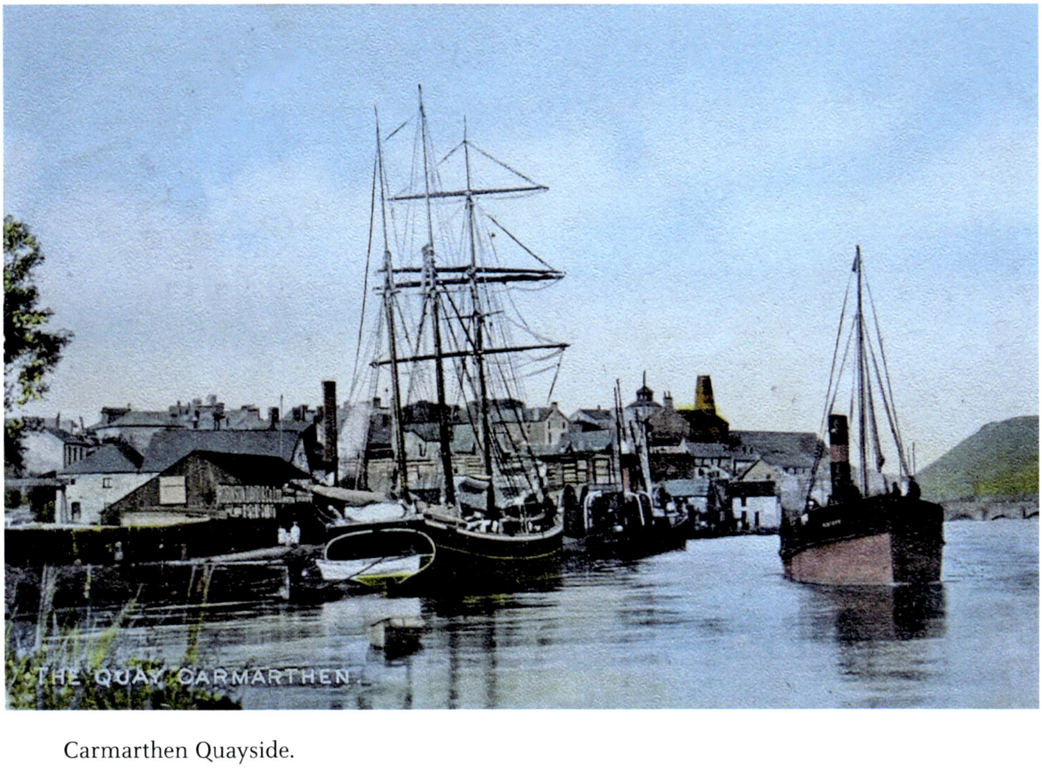

Carmarthen Quayside.

agreed not to export their cheese and distributed some among the locals. When the rioting and threat of further disturbance abated, the mayor withdrew the military. According to the *Carmarthen Journal*, the riot ended with the authorities pleading with the 'lower classes' of the town to be quiet and peaceful, and not to 'insult and outrage' their 'friends or benefactors' any further.

Following years of failing harvests, and a downturn in the iron trade, leading to poor wages, large-scale poverty, and homelessness, Carmarthenshire in the 1830s was suffering agricultural and industrial depression. The government's remedy was twofold. They applied the 1834 Poor Law Amendment Act, which ensured the poor and destitute were housed in workhouses, and the 1835 Highways Act, which allowed landowners to place charges on road users.

This perfect storm of social and economic turmoil created a level of public dissatisfaction so intense that when the tolls came into being, a spectacular demonstration of rebellion erupted, resulting in years of rioting and revolt. Tollgates became symbols of oppression and road users loathed them. They banded together and set out to destroy the county's tollgates and tollhouses. These protests became known as the Rebecca Riots.

Road tolls in one form or another have existed in Britain since turnpikes were introduced in the 1700s. The Industrial Revolution was at its height in the 1830s and Britain's road systems were poor and unable to provide the efficient means of transporting goods and materials required by merchants.

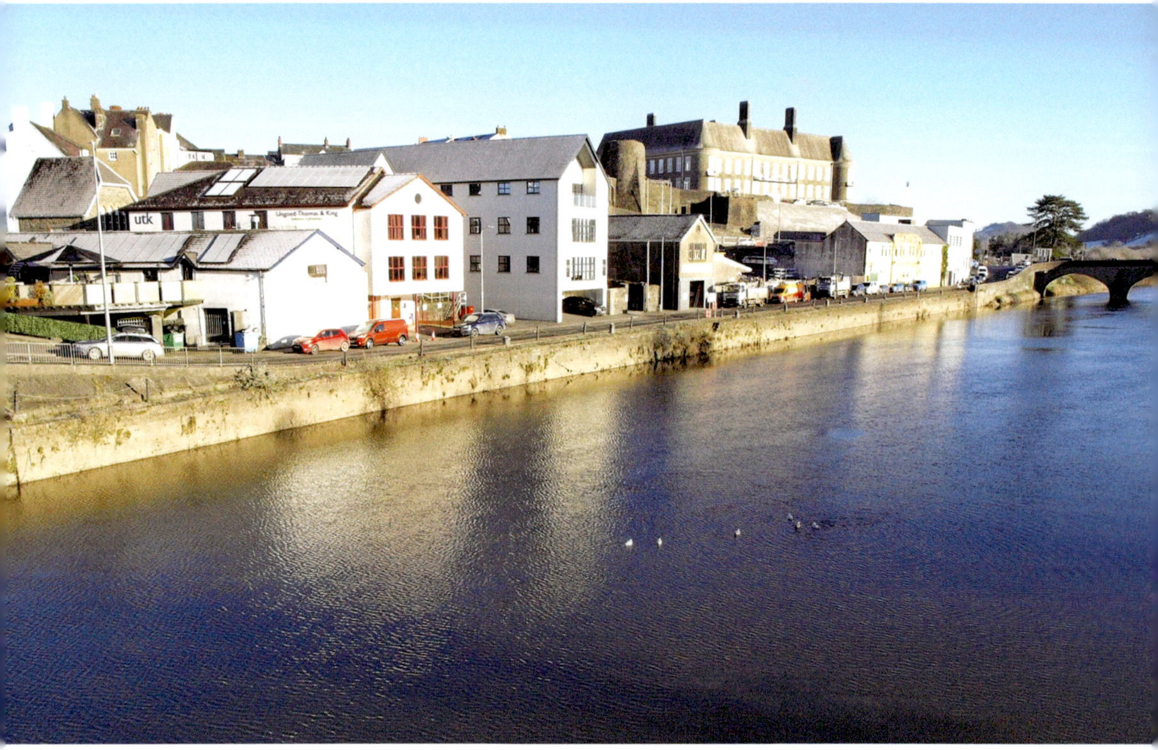

Carmarthen Quayside.

With no national system of highway maintenance, the government introduced the 1835 Highways Act, allowing charges to be imposed for maintaining new roads. Further Acts of Parliament allowed local landowners to create Turnpike Trusts who could build tollgates and bars and set toll charges to pay for the construction and maintenance of new roads.

The number of tollgates within an authority was controlled by trustees, many of whom were landed gentry and magistrates. Usually, one tollgate or bar was erected every 4 miles along major highways. Trustees employed professional toll collectors to raise tolls on their behalf. Unscrupulous toll collectors would take advantage of their position by pocketing tolls, creating additional gates and increasing levies.

Tolls were charged for transporting all goods, including people and animals. The main users of the roads were tenant farmers, agricultural labourers, and farm servants, who often paid tolls twice a day This was in addition to paying rent to their landowners and 10 per cent of their income to the Church.

Frustration turned to anger on the 13 May 1839. Under cover of darkness, a gang of seventy men with blacked up faces and wearing women's bonnets, petticoats and nightgowns arrived at the village of Efailwen, on the Carmarthenshire and Pembrokeshire border. They demolished the newly constructed tollgate and set fire to the tollhouse. The tollgate was replaced only to be torn down a month later by a gang of 400 men dressed as women. It was destroyed again on 17 July by several hundred men wearing women's clothing. What happened at Efailwen stirred the nation and the riots that followed became some of the most famous and spectacular protests in Welsh modern history.

As the riots continued an anonymous leader emerged, known only as Rebecca. It is believed the name was adopted from a bible passage in Genesis 24:60: 'And they blessed Rebecca, and said unto her, "Thou art our sister; he thou the mother of thousands of millions, and let thy seed possess the gate of those which hate them."' Another theory is that Thomas Rees (Twm Carnabwth), the leader of the first riot at Efailwen, borrowed clothes from a woman called Rebecca and the name stuck. His followers became known as his daughters.

Following the attack at Efailwen, farmers held organised meetings where rioters were organised into gangs and targets agreed. On 25 August, near the village of Five Roads, upon the summit of Mynydd Sylen, near Llanelli, a great meeting took place. It attracted over 4,000 supporters.

Two of the most notorious leaders were David Davies, alias 'Dai'r Cantwr', and John Jones, alias 'Shoni Sgubor Fawr'. They and other leaders used the pubs and inns of Five Roads as meeting places, designating the Stag and Pheasant Inn as their headquarters.

During attacks, gang leaders identified themselves by wearing a white cloak and riding a white horse. They carried guns and horns to create noise and confusion, destroyed tollgates, associated properties, and made good their escape. Initially, rioters were careful not to hurt or injure tollkeepers, and frequently helped them to remove property from the tollgate cottage before setting fire to it.

The tollhouse of Glangwili Gate, near Carmarthen, was surrounded by 200 Rebeccaites at 1 a.m. on 25 August. Both house and gate were demolished, and money stolen. The rioting was at its worst in 1843, with two or three attacks occurring daily and tollgates regularly destroyed at Carmarthen and Llanelli. Protesters gradually became more violent, with rioters destroying private property and beating those refusing to comply with their orders.

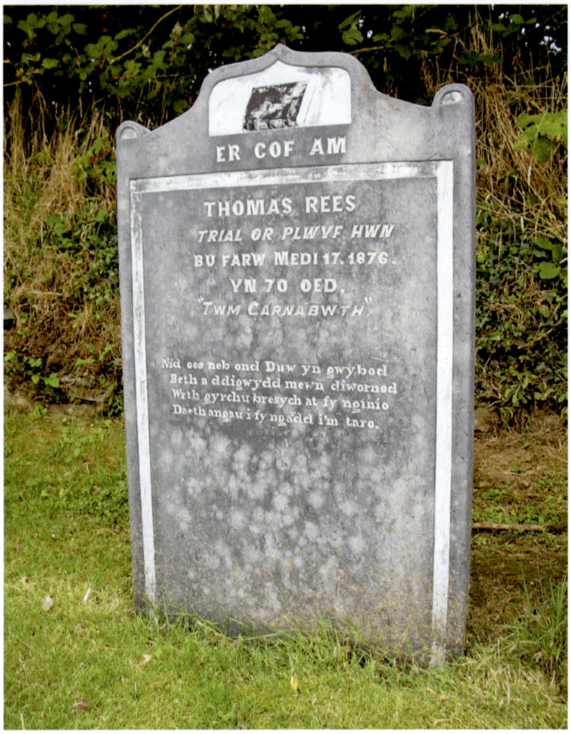

Thomas Rees' grave.

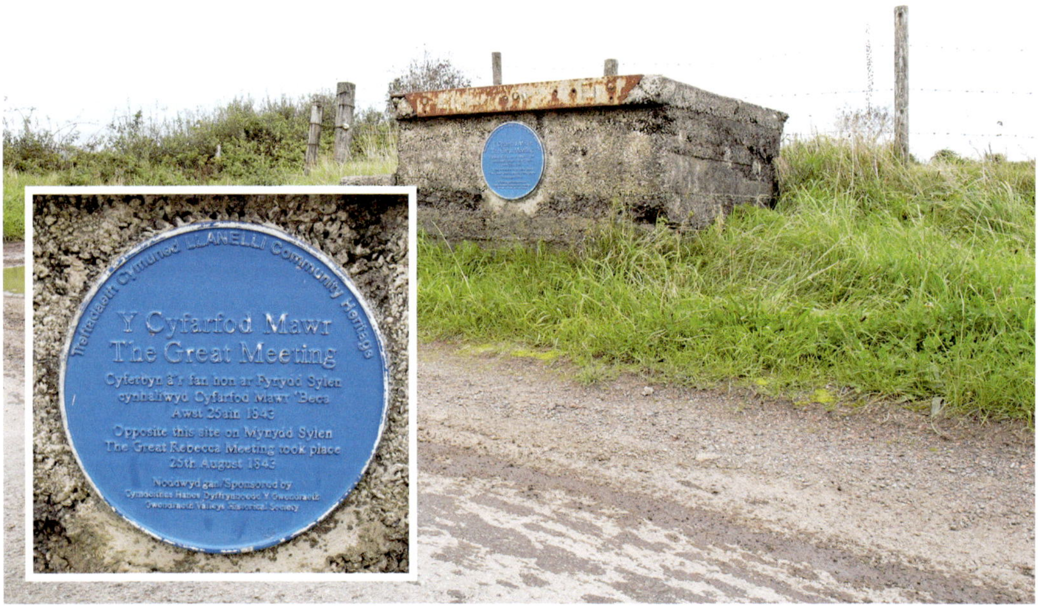

Mynydd Sylen plaque.

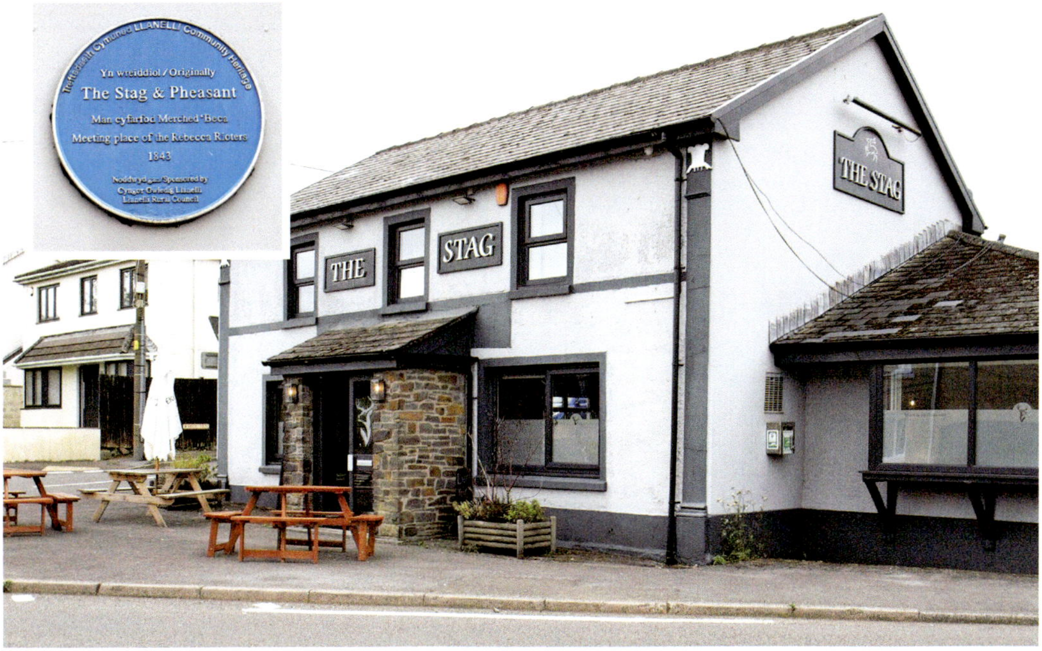

Davies and Jones HQ.

Between 5 and 30 May 1843, tollgates were destroyed at Pontwelly, Carmarthen, Bwlch-y-Clawdd, Llandysul, Pensarn, Nant Gurrey-fach and Llanddarog. As disturbances continued in Carmarthenshire, the government deployed officers from the Metropolitan Police to quash the rebellion and arrest rioters. Two detachments from the Army's 75th and 76th Regiments of Foot, supported by a cavalry squadron from the 4th Royal Irish Dragoon Guards, were also deployed.

In early June, the tollgate at Llanfihangel-ar-Arth was attacked and destroyed by 150 rioters who on 19 June rallied with 1,800 protesters in Carmarthen. This was a turning point. Protesters marched through the town to present a petition to the mayor requesting a reduction in tolls and fees. Their number swelled to over 4,000 as the people, confined by the toll gates encircling the town, joined them.

En route, unruly elements smashed into the Penlan Workhouse. Ransacking it, they threw files, furniture and papers from the windows. A unit of dragoons had arrived in the town the day before and were quickly deployed. Surrounding the workhouse, they began firing at the rioters. There was no escape and those inside had little choice but to surrender. Seventy arrests were made; dozens of prisoners were sentenced to be transported to Australia.

Late on the night of 28 June, Rebecca and her daughters attacked and destroyed the gate and part of the tollhouse. The following night they burnt the Forest Gate tollgate and cottage between Pontardulais and Llaneddi.

During July, gates, bars and tollhouses were destroyed at Pumsaint, Llandilo Rhwnws, Bronvelin, Gwarallt, Porthyrhyd, Pontyberem, Cenarth, and Abergwili. While at Llaneli's

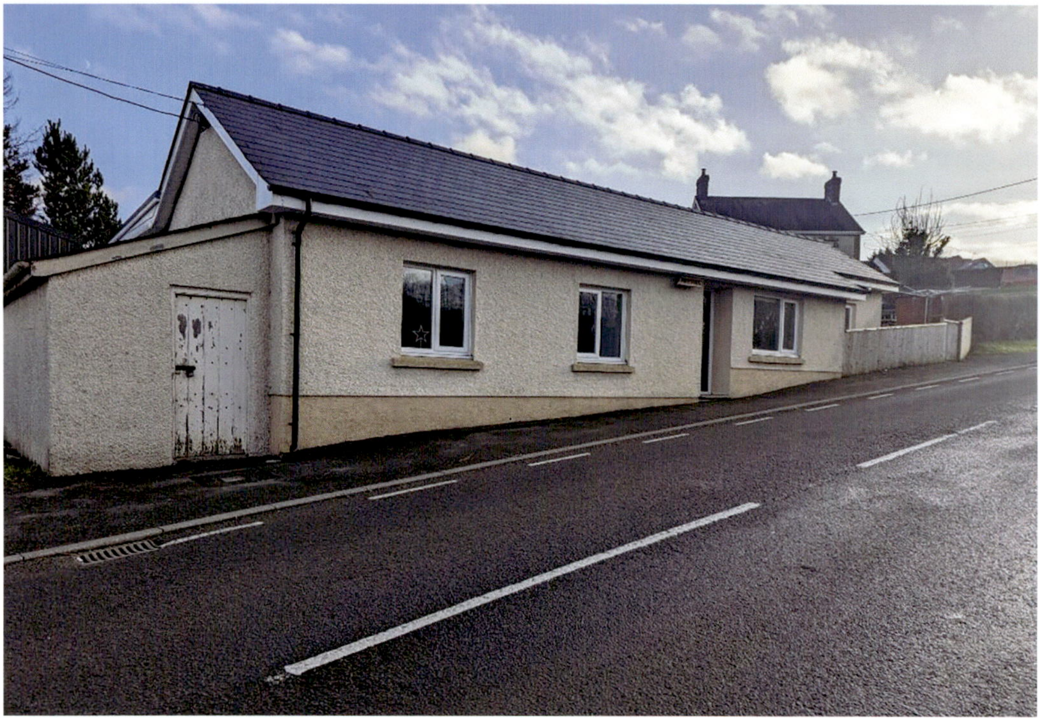

Llanfihangel-ar-Arth Tollhouse.

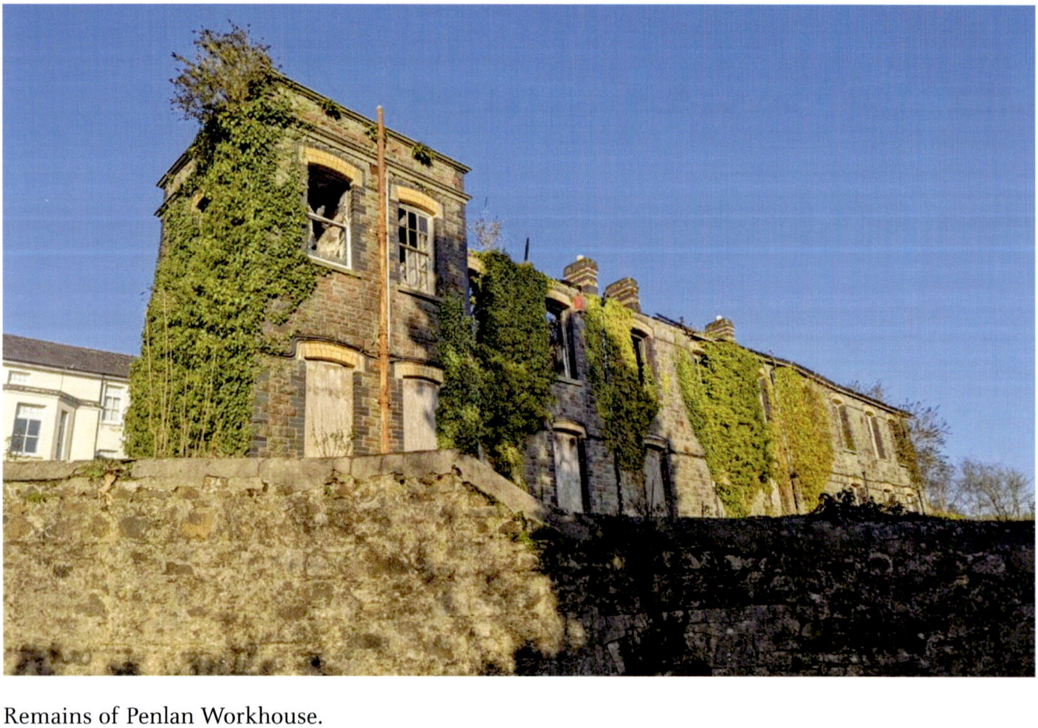

Remains of Penlan Workhouse.

Furnace tollgate, the gatekeeper was beaten, his face blasted by a gun, before the tollgate was destroyed and the tollhouse set alite. Today a blue plaque placed upon the Furnace Post Office, now occupying the site commemorates the incident.

Attacks continued and on 1 August at Pontarllechan the tollbar was destroyed and at Llannon both tollgate and tollhouse were demolished. On the night of 22 August 150 men, mostly on horseback, arrived at Llannon intent on attacking the tollgate. Repeatedly firing their guns, they cheered on their way to the tollgate, which they destroyed in less than ten minutes before tearing down the tollhouse. Local magistrates, along with several policemen, arrived and demanded the rioters to stop and shots were fired. Unperturbed, calling upon each other to be 'true till death,' the men fired at the police, who returned fire. The magistrates called for the Dragoon Guards.

During a fierce exchange, rioters were wounded and captured. The ringleader, John Hughes, a respectable farmer's son and a resident of Llannon, had his horse shot from under him. Despite desperately resisting, he was arrested, having sustained a broken arm and other injuries. Following the fight an express rider raced to hasten the Dragoons. The reassembled rioters continued to fire from the dark before moving, blowing their horns to regroup fleeing comrades. Thirty minutes later, a section of eight Dragoon Guards arrived

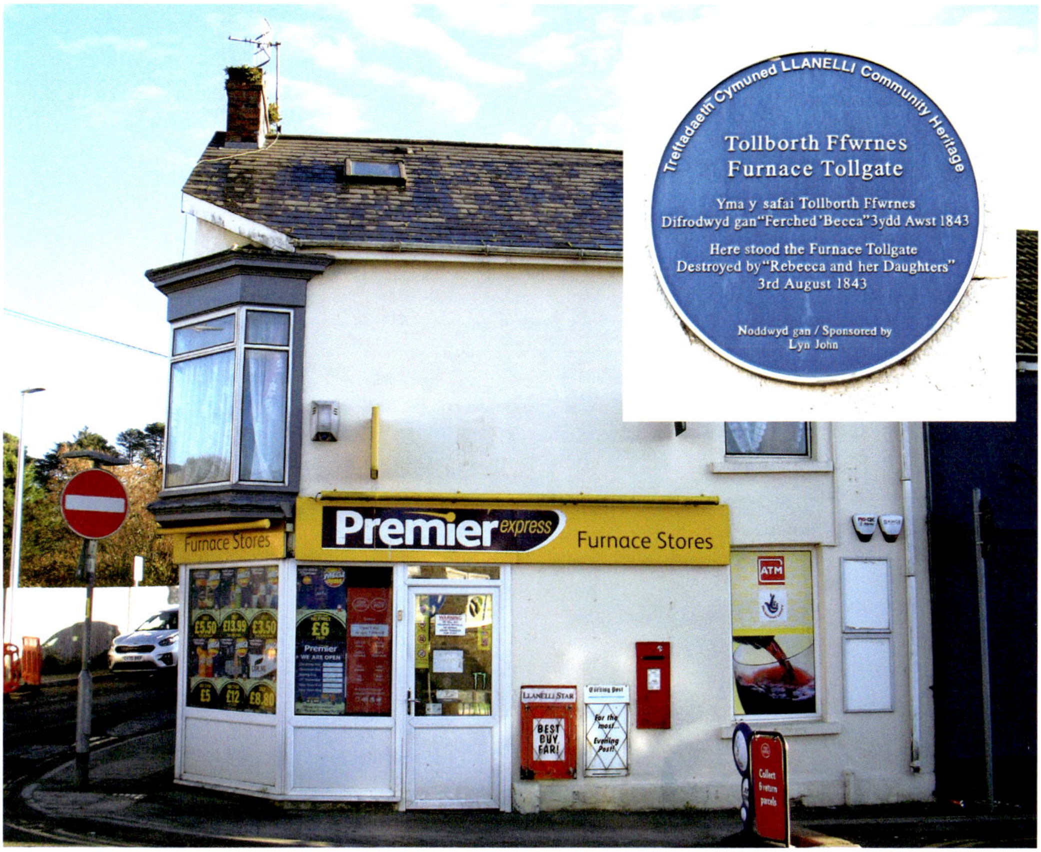

Furnace Post Office.

at the gate. They heard horns coming from all directions in the surrounding hills, but they found no Rebeccaites.

Later, 8 September, well-armed Rebeccaites attacked Sanders Bridge Gate, near Kidwelly, demolishing it. The following night, Davies and Jones were present during an attack on the Hendy tollgate and tollhouse, Llanedi, when seventy-five-year-old tollkeeper Sarah Williams was shot dead. Despite rewards of more than £1,000 being offered for information, nobody was convicted of her murder. Later that month the Metropolitan Police captured David Davies in the Plough and Harrow public house in Five Roads. They handed him over to the Dragoon Guards until his removal to Carmarthen Jail.

The last Rebecca attacks in Carmarthenshire came on 30 September 1843, when rioters removed the Tyrfran tollgate on the road to Felinfoel, dropping it down a nearby coal pit shaft. When the Dragoon Guards, despite being billeted close by at the Union Workhouse, reached the shaft, Rebecca and her daughters had vanished. On 27 December 1843 at Carmarthen Assizes, Davies and Jones, along with thirty-nine rebels, were tried. Davies was sentenced to twenty years' transportation and Jones transportation for life.

Between 1910 and 1912 against the backdrop of industrial conflict now known as 'The Great Unrest', a triple alliance was formed by the National Union of Mineworkers, the National Union of Railwaymen, and the National Transport Workers. This alliance saw the working classes unite in strike action against unfair wages and working conditions.

Llanelli, a regional producer of tinplate, had established export links around the globe, and was a vibrant and commercially successful town with three small docks. Below the

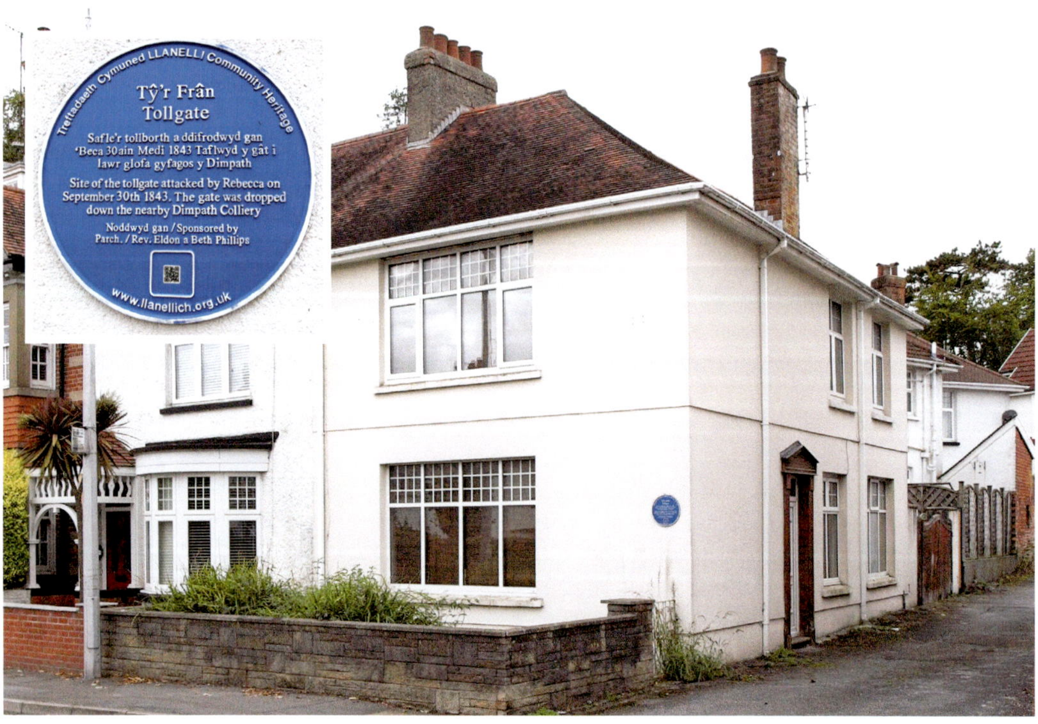

Site of Tyrfran Tollgate.

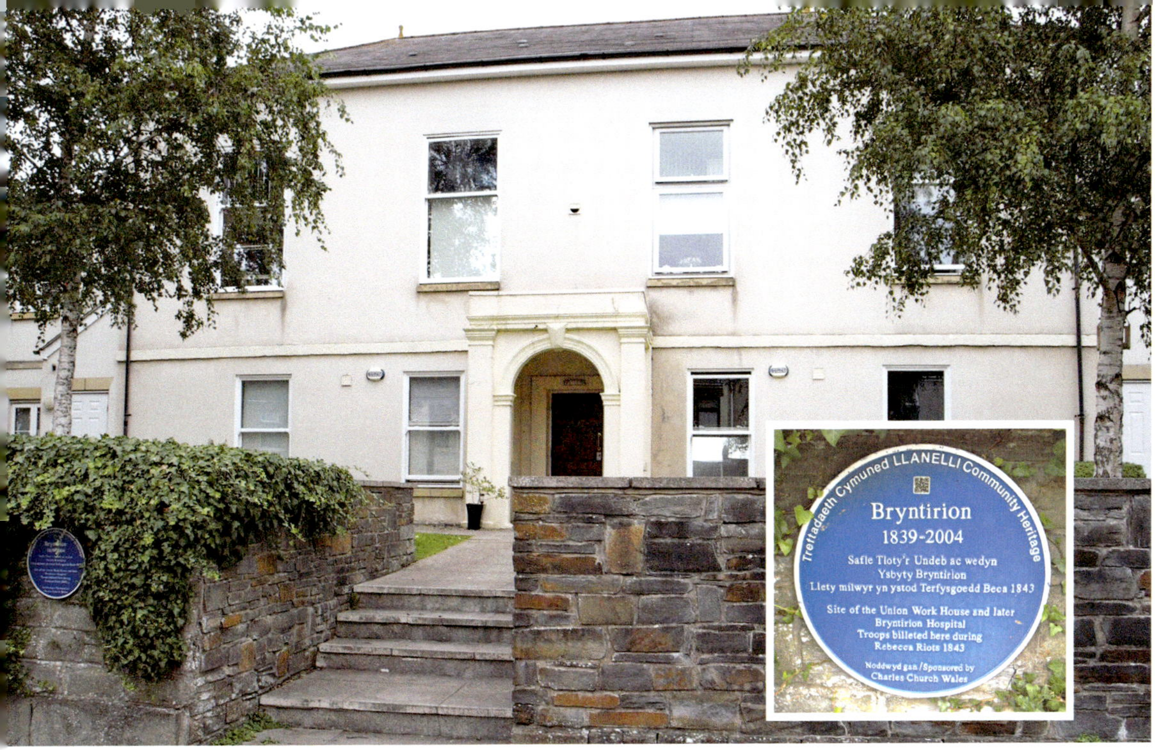

Union Workhouse.

surface of its industrial achievements, disaster was unfolding. Minimal healthcare, poor sanitation, deprivation, insecure employment, and low wages were generating tensions, agitation and a loathing of the state that would lead to rebellion and riot.

Miners at nearby Trimsaran went on strike during 1911, demanding a minimum wage to combat the cost-of-living crises. Wages had not risen since 1900. Furious at the huge profits being made by railway companies, facing low wages and enforced overtime, railway workers in towns and cities across the UK went on strike for the first time.

At Llanelli on 17 August 1911, 500 rail workers held a two-day strike that ended in riot when 4,500 local coal miners and tin workers picketed the gates at the town's two main level crossings. Tonypandy and Cardiff police forces were also policing strike action and requested support from Llanelli Police. This support left Llanelli's police force with just twenty officers.

At 5.00 a.m. on 18 August, Thomas Jones, a local grocer, councillor, magistrate, and a shareholder in the Great Western Railway, met with strikers to break the strike. Realising he could not help, and fearing for the town's safety, he called for military aid. A detachment of 370 men of the North Lancashire Regiment commanded by Captain Burrows arrived from Cardiff at 7.45 a.m. to render assistance. Following negotiations with union leaders, several trains carrying live cattle and mail were allowed through on compassionate grounds, and relationships between strikers and the military remained amicable. Despite this, both representatives of Great Western Railway and Jones were unhappy that the presence of troops had not broken the strike. They called for reinforcements to attend Llanelli. On 19 August, soldiers of the Worcestershire Regiment arrived under the command of Major

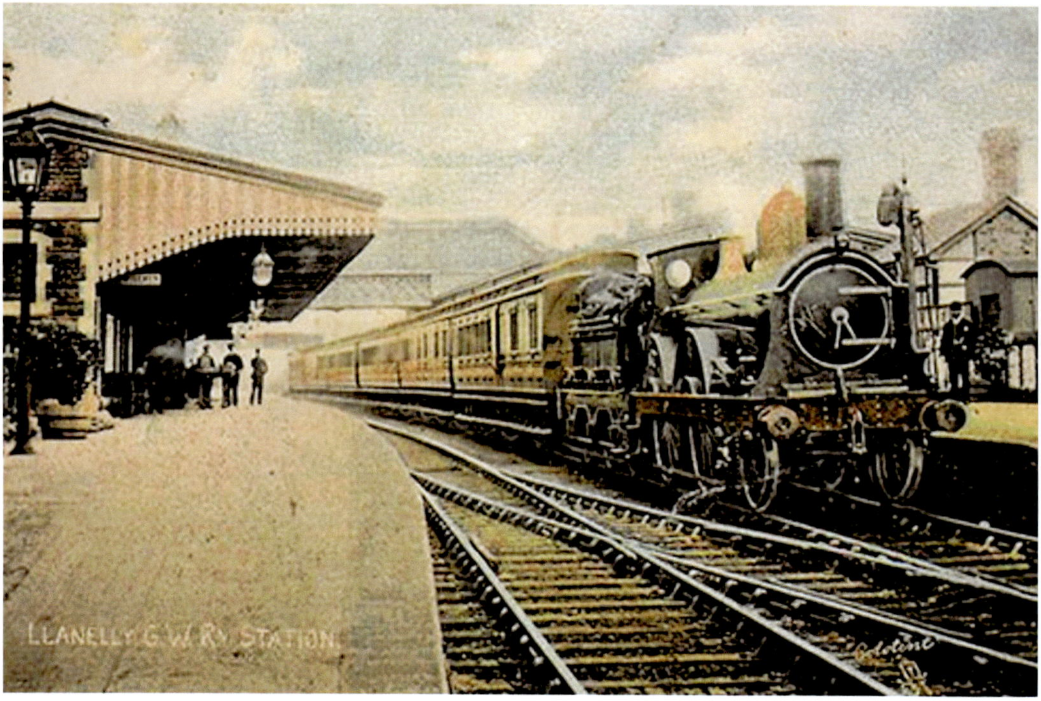

Brownlow Stuart, and negotiations took place in the Town Hall. During the meeting picketers stopped a passenger train. In response, Stuart ordered his troops to fix bayonets, and when picketers refused to move, he ordered them to bayonet charge the crowd.

With the crossing clear, the train began moving, chased by strikers who climbed aboard the engine and stopped it in a railway cutting. When Stuart's troops arrived, strikers lining the top of the cutting began hurling rocks at them. Stuart ordered his soldiers to open fire on the protestors. One picketer called out, 'It's all right! It's blanks boys! Don't move, they won't shoot.'

But the soldiers did shoot, killing local tinplate worker John 'Jac' John (twenty-one), a gifted rugby player with the Llanelli Oriental Stars. Leonard Worsell (nineteen), who was recuperating from TB, also died. Worsell was shaving when, having heard the commotion, went to his garden to watch, and was hit by a stray bullet.

The Worcestershire Regiment and police withdrew to the railway station and a full-scale riot erupted that lasted the night. During an attack on the railway station, every window was smashed and its tracks torn up. Rioters looted goods vans and set fire to ninety-six coal trucks and hay waggons The ferocious flames were visible 5 miles away.

In full view of the army and police, Mayor Jones's grocer's shop was attacked, and a freight wagon packed with explosive detonators set on fire. At 11.30 p.m., the wagon exploded, killing four bystanders. The magnitude of the explosion rocked the town.

The police and army, with bayonets fixed, began clearing the railway sidings of rioters who fled, smashing shops before attacking the Town Hall. Pitched battles between pickets, policemen and soldiers increased. The army erected a field hospital at the Station Hotel for victims.

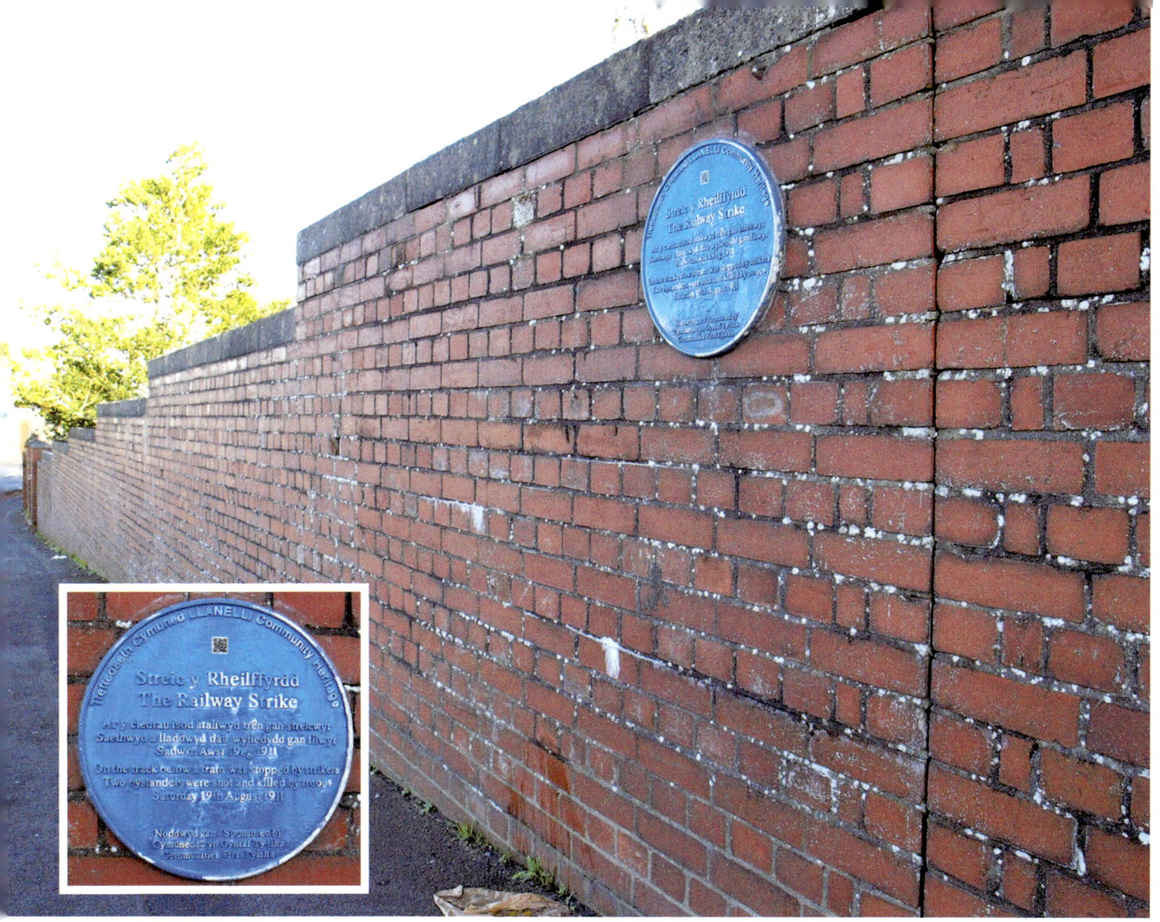

Union Bridge, Queen Victoria Road.

A battalion of the Royal Sussex Regiment arrived in Llanelli under the command of Major Ernest, Henry Montresor, bringing the number of troops in the town to around 1,000. Montresor immediately ordered his troops to fix bayonets, and they began clearing the streets of rioters.

The strike ended bitterly and bloodily, with the 'Battle of Market Street' where many rioters suffered serious injuries. At the coroner's inquest into the two deaths witnesses gave evidence that stones were not thrown and that the military had made a mistake. It was also alleged that when Major Stuart instructed magistrate Henry Wilkins to read the Riot Act, he failed to do so effectively and unwillingly mumbled his way through it. Despite this and other evidence that was detrimental to the military, the coroner delivered a verdict of justifiable homicide.

5

Adventurers and Explorers

Carmarthenshire has its fair share of home-grown military personalities. Some have achieved impressive feats in battle, while others have shown remarkable courage, endurance, and perseverance in times of great adversity. All have stood in harm's way for what they believed in. This chapter considers some of Carmarthenshire's courageous and notable personalities.

The Phillips family of Abergwili, near Carmarthen, are unmatched in their contribution to defending the realm.

John George Philipps (1783–1869) entered the Royal Navy in May 1796, during the French Revolutionary War (1792–1802) and the Napoleonic War (1803–15), becoming an accomplished sailor and captain. He served as a midshipman on HMS *Minotaur* fighting with great distinction alongside Nelson's flagship HMS *Vanguard* at the Battle of the Nile (1798). He also saw action on land during the capture of Naples, and the Port of Rome, as well as the siege of Genoa, and in land operations in Egypt during 1801.On 22 October 1814 he was promoted to commander and following his retirement became a magistrate and then Deputy-Lieutenant for Carmarthen.

John's brother Captain Griffith Grismond Philipps (1822–91) was a highly decorated captain in the Welch Fusiliers, who fought in the Peninsular Wars (1807–14) and with great distinction at the Battle of Waterloo (1815). Griffith Grismond Philipps (1811–91), John's son, was a naval hero whose remarkable exploits are believed to be the inspiration for C. S. Forester's fictional naval hero Horatio Hornblower.

In 1825, at the age of fourteen, John entered naval service as a first-class volunteer. In 1827, as midshipman on HMS *Dartmouth* he fought in the Greek War of Independence (1821–29), taking part in the Battle of Navarino (1827) and destroying the Ottoman fleet anchored in Navarino bay, Greece. He received the Navarino medal and clasp for his gallant actions and heroism. This battle is notable as being the last major engagement involving only wooden sailing ships.

On 28 June 1838, he received his commission to lieutenant and saw active service in the Royal Navy's West Africa Squadron suppressing the slave trade in Africa. He took part in breathtaking adventures, pursuing, engaging, and boarding Arab dhows (traditional sailing vessels), and was mentioned in reports for his enthusiasm and prudence.

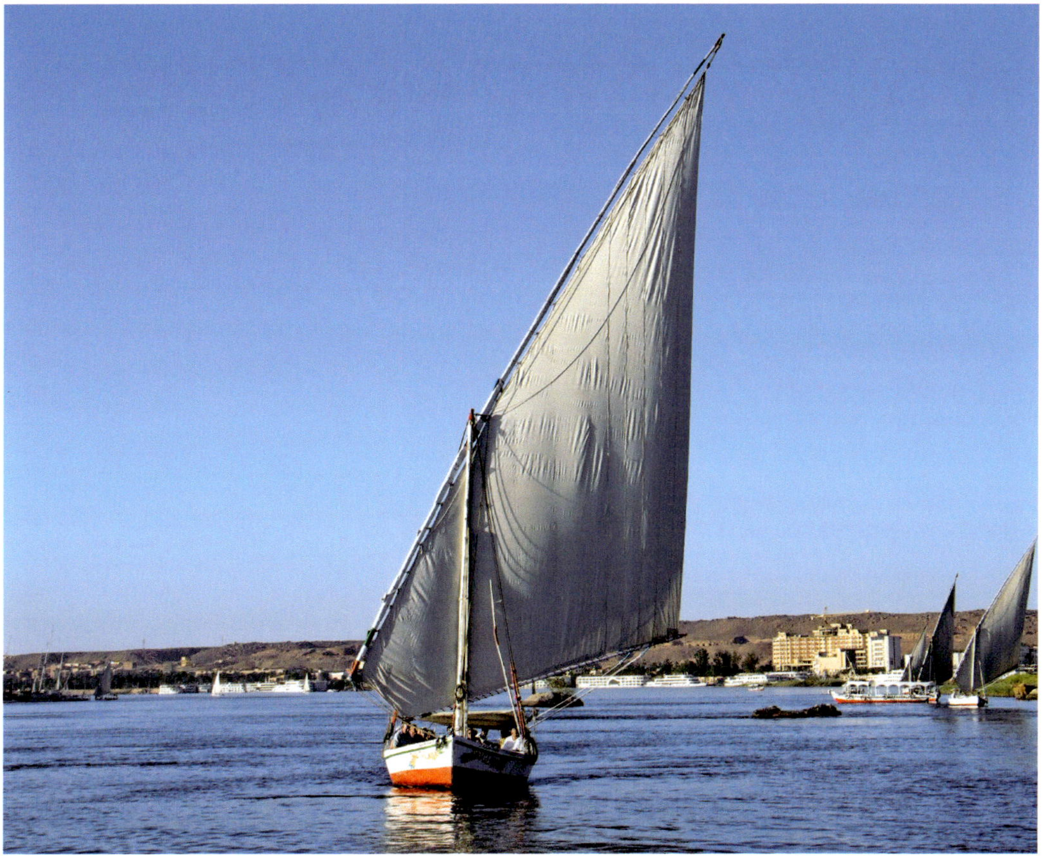

A traditional dhow boat.

John saw service in the Crimean War (1853–56), landing British troops at Kalimite and taking part in the siege of Sebastopol. He received the Crimean medal with Sebastopol clasp for this. He retired in 1856 at the rank of commander and at the time of his death was the last survivor of the Battle of Navarino. His funeral took place in St David's churchyard, Carmarthen.

Another noteworthy family are the Edwardes family of Rhyd-y-gors. Between the family they held high office in both town and county, including high sheriff of the county, four occasions as mayor, and six as the town sheriff, and have a long history of serving with merit as high-ranking officers in the British Army and Royal Navy.

Brothers Captain David John Edwardes (1787–1866) and Captain Henry Lewis Edwardes (1788–1866) were courageous men. David served with the Royal Horse Artillery in the Peninsula War (1808–14) in 1813, and fought at Vitoria, San Sebastian, Nive, Neville and at the Battle of Waterloo (1815). Henry also served in the Napoleonic wars with the 62nd (Wiltshire) Regiment of Foot. He was related by marriage to General Picton. Both had distinguished military careers, noted for valour and daring exploits. Henry is credited with bringing the recipe for Worcestershire Sauce back from India. At the family's place of worship in St Mary's Church, Llanllwch, are two memorials attached to the wall behind

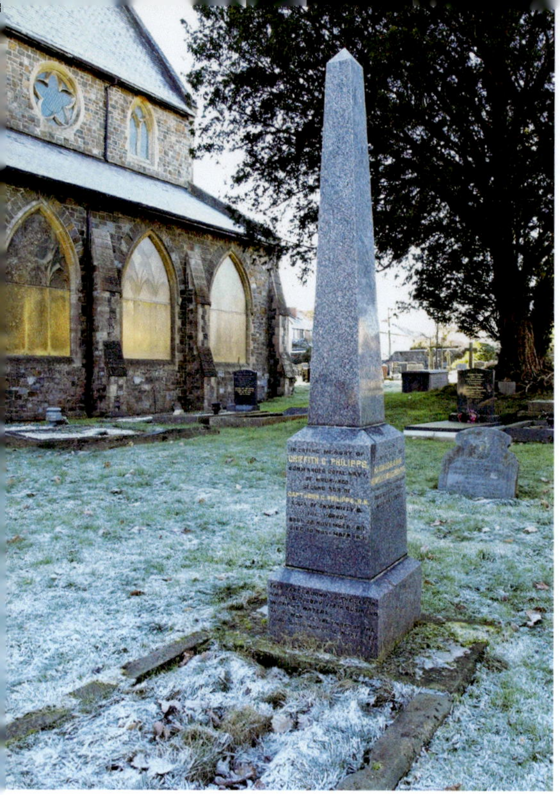

Memorial to Captain Grismond Philipps.

the family's front pew. Several of the family are interred there in the family vault, which lies beneath the floor under the pew.

Many of Carmarthenshire's sons have fought in historic battles, but John William Jones Davies has the distinction of being the only one to die fighting Zulu warriors at the disastrous Battle of Isandlwana during the Anglo-Zulu War (1879).

Born at Uplands, Llandefaelog, in 1849 to Edward and Maria Davies, John joined the Brecon-based 24th (2nd Battalion Warwickshire) Regiment of Foot in 1867 as a private service number 743. At the time of the battle the bulk of the 2nd Battalion, accompanied by Lord Chelmsford, were several miles away from Isandlwana. John was part of G Company, 170 men under the command of Lieutenant Pope, who were attached, along with a contingent of 500 Natal troops, to the men of the 1st Battalion of the 24th.

On the afternoon of 22 January, 20,000 Zulu warriors fell upon the British camp at Isandlwana. Many Zulus were killed by artillery grapeshot and sustained rifle fire. The British forces resisted for over an hour, firing volley after volley of bullets into the approaching Zulus until their ammunition ran low. Unable to break the British lines and losing men, the Zulus retreated. But when the British fire faltered, during their retreat, they pressed on. The battle ended in frantic hand-to-hand fighting and, eventually, the Zulu warriors overran the British camp.

During the battle, Lord Chelmsford repeatedly disregarded desperate messages requesting relief and did not arrive with reinforcements until nightfall. Chelmsford spent an anxious night close to the battlefield in expectation of being attacked aware that they were too late. John William Jones Davies was amongst the hundreds of stripped and mutilated soldiers.

Chelmsford ordered his men to leave before the light of dawn, fearing his troops would be demoralised by seeing the terrible fate of their comrades. Following the war, Zulu testimony stated that at Isandlwana 300 Natal troops ran away, but the red-coated men of the 24th stood their ground and fought bravely to the last man. Over 1,300 soldiers were killed. The Zulus themselves lost between 1,000 to 2,500 men. In 1881, the 24th were retitled the South Wales Borderers, and are now part of the Royal Welsh armoured infantry regiment A beautiful memorial plaque to John sits within St Maelog's Church in Llanfaelog.

Another man with an unusual contribution to the county's military heritage is Petty Officer Francis Dunn from Llanelli, a caulker's mate on HMS *Erebus*. This was one of two ships of Rear-Admiral Sir John Franklin's 1845 ill-fated expedition to locate the Northwest Passage.

Francis was 5 feet 9 inches, had a fresh complexion, hazel eyes, and deep brown hair. He joined the Royal Navy in Malta on 6 October 1843 and served as a carpenter on the thirty-six-gun frigate HMS *Belvidera* until 1845. On 27 March, he was selected to join HMS *Erebus*. Each of the 129 officers selected were handpicked for their seamanship, specialist skills, and previous displays of courage.

The *Erebus* and HMS *Terror* became icebound off King William Land for two years whilst searching for a safe Northwest Passage. Eventually, around 100 crew members abandoned the safety of their vessels to trek 900 miles, across frozen wastes, to safety.

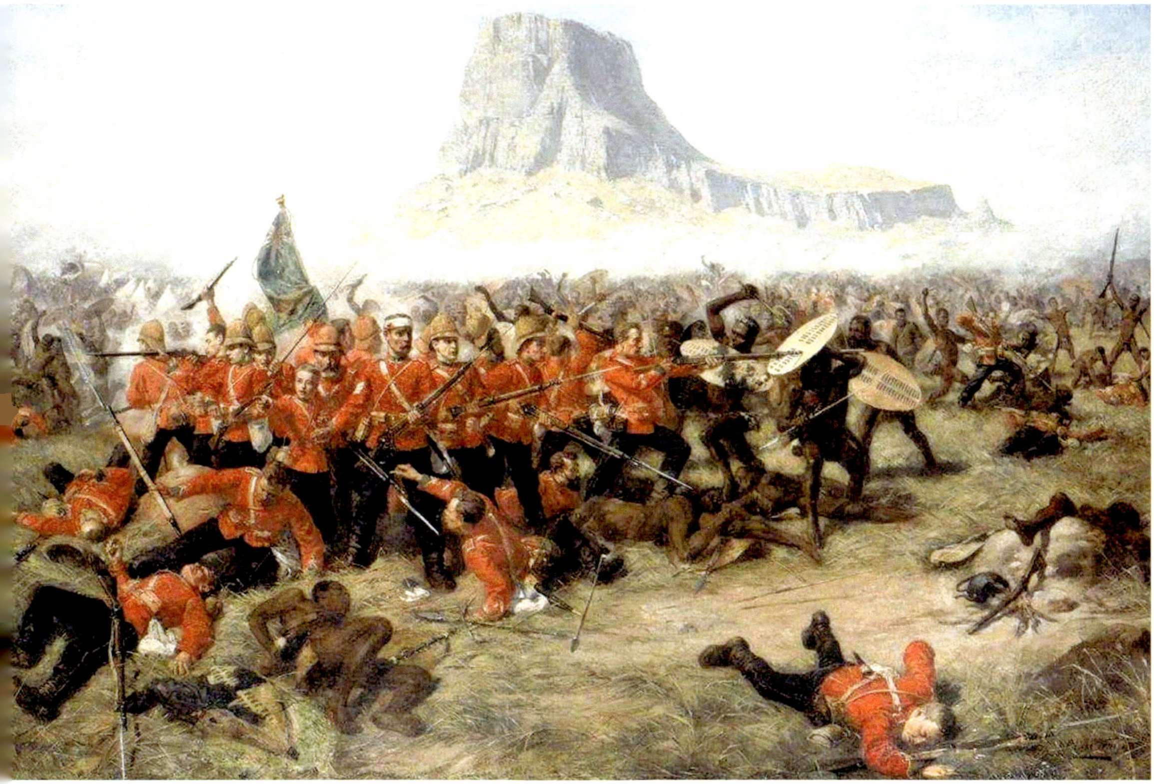

Battle of Isandlwana, Charles Edwin Fripp.

The exact end of the intrepid crew members is unknown. Historians, archaeologists, and scientists have tried to piece together the crew's fate from evidence found by subsequent expeditions, explorers, scientists, and interviews with local Inuit people.

Their consensus suggests the men were already suffering from lead poisoning when they left the ships, a result of their water distillation system and badly soldered food cans. Many died crossing King William Island and evidence suggests they resorted to cannibalism. Between thirty and forty reached the northern end of the Adelaide Peninsula on the Canadian mainland, but all died of starvation, scurvy, or exposure.

The failure of this military led scientific expedition led some experts to view the voyage as a disaster, and Rear Admiral Franklin a failure. Alternative opinions paid tribute to the dangers and perils the men faced, the terror and misery they endured, locked in the ice with no hope of rescue. Whatever happened, it required the men to act with courage, fortitude, and heroism. To behave otherwise would have resulted in a breakdown of military discipline and abandoning the ships much earlier than they did.

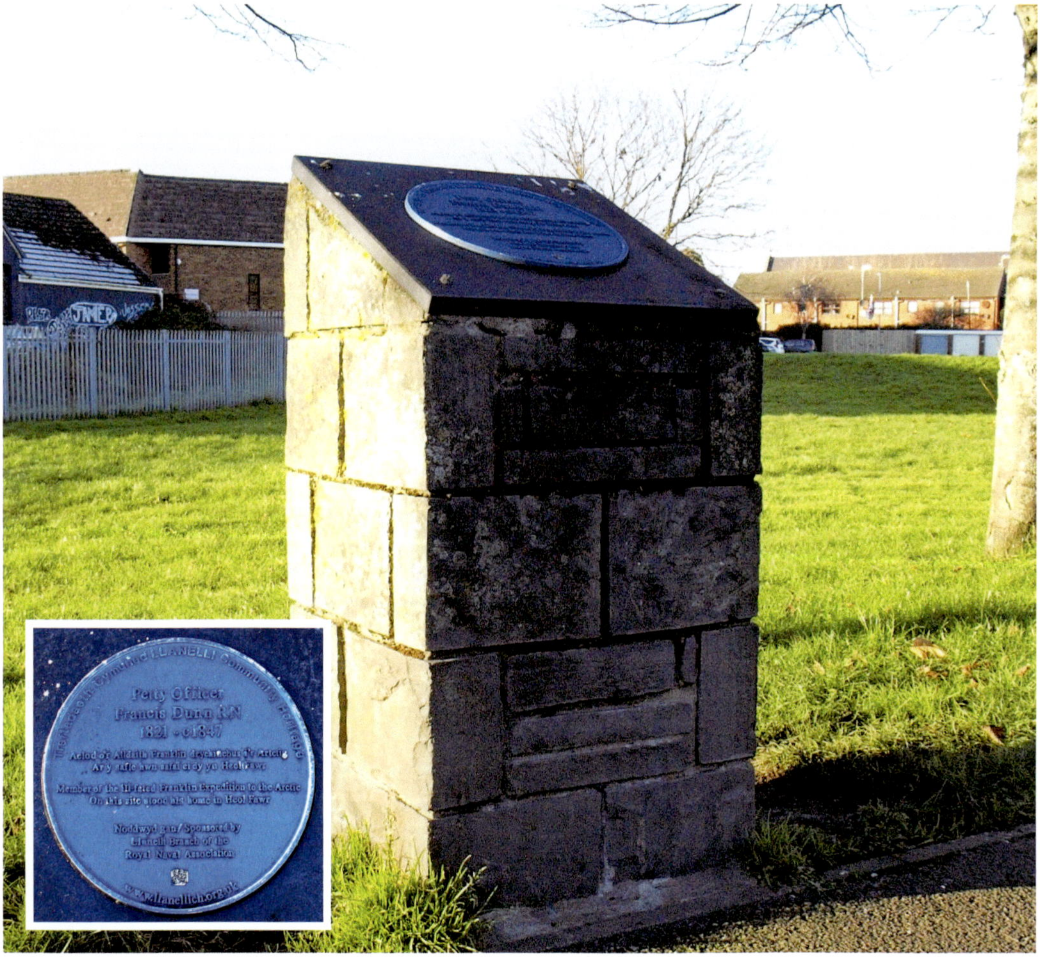

Memorial to Petty Officer Francis Dunn, Glanmor Road.

Tom Davies was born in July 1918 at Dryslwyn to James and Martha Davies. Before he was called up for military service in 1940, he was an office clerk. Unhappy and confined by clerical life, he yearned for freedom and adventure. Both would come and go in May 1941 when serving with the Royal Artillery on the island of Crete.

On 20 May 1940, Germany attacked Crete. After twelve days of fighting 4,000–6,000 Allied troops and around 6,000 Axis troops were dead and further 5,000 Allied troops taken as prisoners of war (POW). Among them was Tom Davies, who, following a gruelling three-day march in the searing Mediterranean heat, arrived at a hastily constructed prison camp at Maleme Aerodrome. Tom and another young soldier made their escape, already weakened by dysentery, but after a couple of days in the stifling heat, with no food and water, the other man became ill. Tom refused to leave him and spent several days dragging, carrying, and pulling his comrade back to the prison, where, sadly, they were recaptured.

After a few days rest, the spirited Tom escaped again. While free he realised that he was putting people helping him in danger. Detection was unavoidable on such a small island; he handed himself in.

Tom volunteered when the men were given the opportunity to work for extra food. The task was grim, burying over 4,000 German soldiers who had laid in the blistering sun for days and weeks.

Tom was among the last to leave Crete on an overcrowded, diseased riddled vessel bound for Salonika, Greece. The POWs were billeted in an old army barracks for several days with no food and little water and eventually herded into cramped cattle boxes, with just a small, barred window for ventilation, and transported to Stalag 18, a POW camp in Wolfsberg, Austria.

Tom spent three years as a POW in Austria, working in different camps, doing hard labour. Battling recurrences of malaria, he witnessed brutal and degrading treatment of Russian POWs and the experiments by Nazi scientist determined to show the supremacy of Germans as a 'master race'.

His time in Austria ended when he and two other POWs escaped. They were captured two weeks later in Hungary and Tom went to the Sajmište concentration and extermination camp, Zemun Belgrade. In this atrocious place he witnessed unbelievable horrors and brutal treatment of civilians and POWs. Some of the greatest tragedy and horrors Tom experienced here came when Allied bombs inadvertently landed on the camp.

It was during one bombing raid that Tom finally made good an escape. Reaching Yugoslavia, he fought with partisans until he was recaptured. Escaping, yet again, he rejoined other POWs fighting with the resistance movement. At last, by pure luck, on 20 July 1944, Tom and five other POWs unexpectedly found themselves on a plane with a group of wounded partisans heading for the safety of Italy.

Tom was awarded the Military Medal in recognition of his wartime service and bravery displayed in battle when he arrived back in Britain. A distinguished son, he deserves the title of the 'Great Escapee', having escaped five times from four POW camps. Tom lived to be 101, passing away in April 2020.

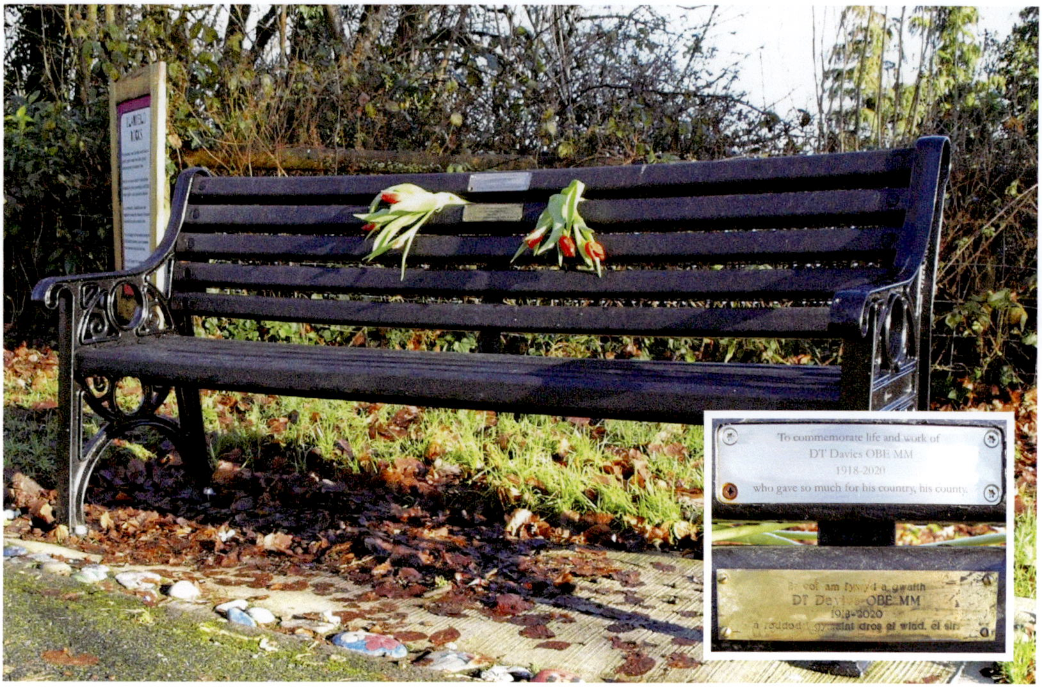

Memorial bench, Penlan Park Dryslwyn.

The Angel of Ciao

Jane Evans is one of the county's little-known and unsung daughters, whose escapades rank alongside the best female Victorian adventures of her time. She was born at Ty Muaux Ciao, close to the Dolaucothi Gold Mines.

Jane and her four brothers were stuck in poverty as both parents had died. In 1854, when she was aged fifteen, her older brother Griffith sold her to a widowed neighbour. She fled, rather than wed.

She'd never left her village before, but followed her cousin's drive of cattle, horses, pigs, sheep, and geese to London. It was not long before she was discovered, and her cousin let her join the safety of the drove. Jane dressed appropriately, learnt how to drive livestock, and led sections of the drove on horseback as it wound its way through Wales and southern England. The long journey was physically hard, fraught with dangers, and she endured many hardships and bleak events.

When the drove was completed, her cousin introduced her to the Reverend and Lady Alicia Blackwood. They were travelling to Turkey to assist Florence Nightingale tend wounded soldiers of the Crimean War (1853–56). Jane joined Lady Blackwood, her husband and another young woman going to Constantinople (today Istanbul). Nightingale was an extremely focused nurse and her opinion of ladies who came out to assist the hospitals was low. Florence, who had no qualification herself, directed Lady Blackwood with the help of Jane and their other female companion to create and manage an unofficial hospital for the wives, widows, and children of soldiers in the cities Scutari district.

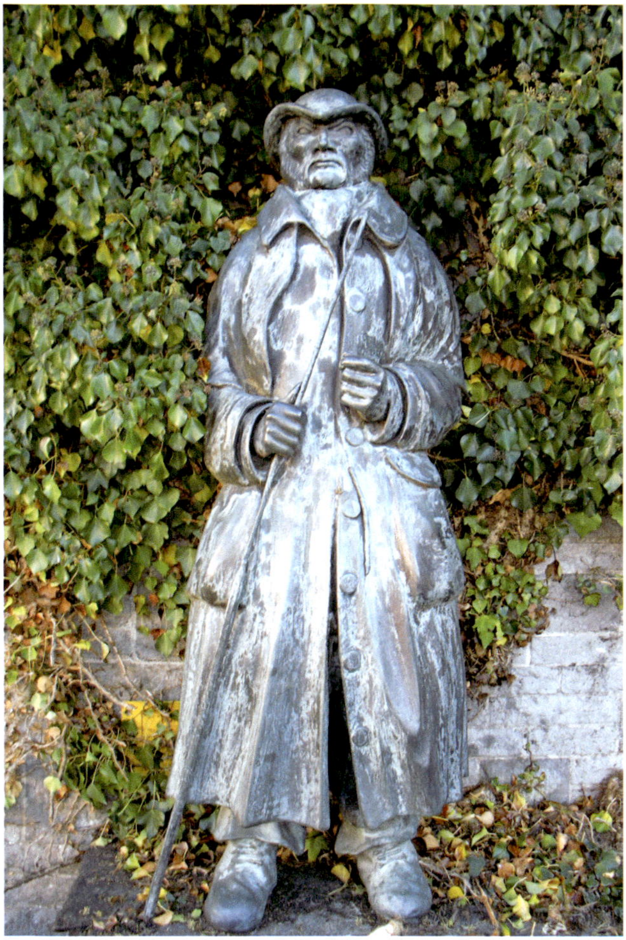

Drovers Statue, near Tourist Information Centre, Llandovery.

The three women readily accepted the task, and in time Jane was asked to tend to the wounded soldiers in the General Military Hospital. Jane asked if she could wear a nurse's uniform, but Florence refused, stating that she was not a nurse, only a helper. During this time, Jane witnessed appalling scenes, horrendous injuries, great suffering, and much death. The hospital was filthy, filled with vermin and overflowing with patients. Many men were still covered in battlefield mud and blood, while others were suffering from fever, dysentery, and cholera.

As time passed, Florence became increasingly impressed by Jane's ability to care for the sick, injured and dying. In 1855, she took a team of nurses to inspect medical facilities near the front lines and requested Jane and Lady Blackwood to join as nurses. They witnessed unsanitary wards infected with rodents and cellars full of unburied soldiers. Those still alive had lice, maggots crawled through their wounds, and many were riddled with secondary illnesses.

During her time in the Crimea, Jane met and collaborated with fellow Welsh nurse Betsi Cadwaladr, and together they battled inhuman conditions, bringing relief and hope to those they treated.

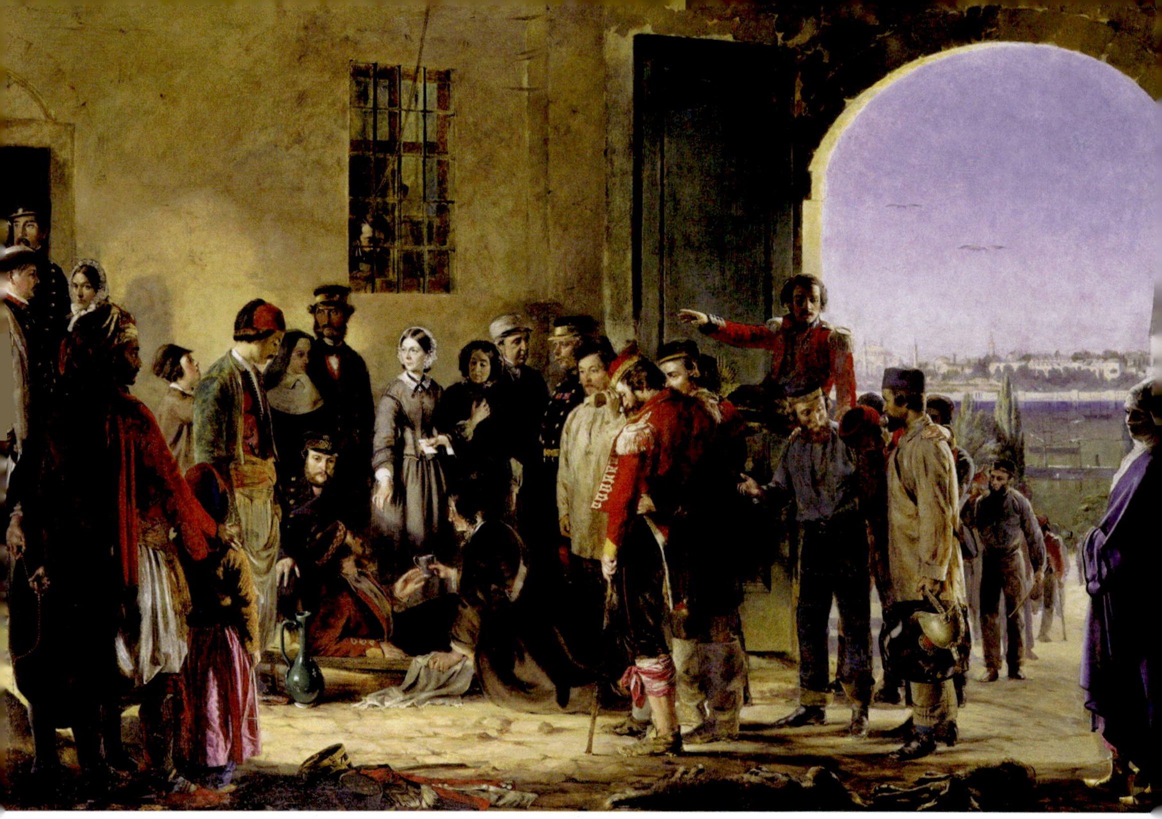

Wounded being received at Scutari. (Wellcome Collection)

Nightingale finally realised Jane was up to par and asked her to run the General Hospital in Balaclava until the war ended and she returned home. Buoyed by her experiences in the Crimean War, Jane arrived home in Wales, apprehensive about her reception. Her forebodings were correct. Some residents were excited, others were not. There was no hero's welcome for her, as with many of Florence's nurses. Refusing to move in and look after her brothers, Jane lived out her days alone in a small cottage. Jane's return may have been uneventful, and her story may have become lost had it not been for the work of Christine Purkis, whose historical novel *Jane Evans* fictionalises her hitherto unknown story of Wales's first woman to lead a drove.

6

Heroes and Heroism

This chapter is dedicated to the bravery, self-sacrifice, and heroism of some of the better- and lesser-known military men, women, and civilians associated with the county.

Not all acts of military heroism are performed in the heat of battle or in foreign lands; heroes come from all levels of society. For example, the fourteen civilian munitions workers at Pembrey who, despite being in shock, severely burnt and injured following an explosion at the factory in 1918, saved lives, stopped the spread of fire, and moved ordnance to safety. They were deservedly awarded the Medal of the Order of the British Empire for acts of heroism and bravery.

Amongst them were telephonist Violet Annie Davies (fifteen), who unwaveringly remained at her post, and Jane Fisher (fifty-five) and May Evans (twenty-six), who helped move munitions and prevented fire spreading, risking their own lives. Other heroes were not so lucky. Edith Copham (nineteen), Mary Fitzmaurice (thirty-six) and Jane Jenkins (twenty-one) were killed while attempting to make a bomb safe. All three were buried with military style honours.

Wales's warrior Princess Gwenllian personifies the spirit of Wales as a nation – wild, beautiful, patriotic, and courageous. Likened by many historians to the Celtic warrior Boadicea, Gwenllian is the only woman known to have led a Welsh army into battle during the medieval period.

The daughter of Gruffydd ap Cynan (1055–1137), King of Gwynedd, north-west Wales, and his wife, Angharad. Her passion for Welsh patriotism was strengthened by her father, who trained her in the art of war. Gwenllian became proficient in sword, bow, and lance and an exceptional horse rider.

Physically striking, with long, flaming red hair and deep blue eyes, at thirteen, she met Gruffydd ap Rhys, Prince of Deheubarth. The pair fell in love and eloped to Gruffydd's castle, in Dinefwr in the Tywi Valley, where they had four sons: Morgan, Maelgwyn, Maredudd and Rhys.

Gwenllian and Gruffydd raided Norman locations throughout Deheubarth (South Wales) antagonising their Norman foes, redistributing seized goods and wealth among the local population. Despite Norman prowess, the pair evaded detection.

When King Henry I of England died in December 1135, Welsh Lord of Brycheiniog, Hywel ap Maredudd, led a revolt against Maurice de Londres, Lord of Kidwelly. The two sides met at Llwchwr, Swansea, where Maredudd's army defeated the Norman lord who fled back to Kidwelly Castle. Believing the Normans routed, Gruffydd rode north to secure the forces of Gwenllian's father to reinforce his own, to drive the routed Normans out of Deheubarth.

In late February 1136, Gwenllian's spies reported the Normans were assembling at Kidwelly Castle. Having made sure her younger sons Maredudd and Rhys were safe, Gwenllian rallied men in the Tywi Valley to defend their lands.

Gwenllian and her sons, Maelgwyn and Morgan, arrived at Kidwelly Castle with 200 ill-equipped men. As the daylight failed, she made camp in nearby woodland to the north of the castle and waited for her husband to arrive. She planned to deploy her troops in guerrilla hit-and-run style raids.

She split her forces. One group remained with her at their woodland camp, ready to cut-off supplies destined for Maurice de Londres, while the other group, led by a local chieftain, Gruffydd ap Llewellyn, went by boat to engage Norman forces attempting to land along the coast.

Gruffydd ap Llewellyn betrayed Gwenllian. He met Maurice de Londres and told him about her plans and where she was camped. Maurice de Londres led his Norman army from Kidwelly Castle, unseen along the banks of the River Gwendraeth Fach. Once he'd surrounded Gwenllian's camp, he launched a surprise attack.

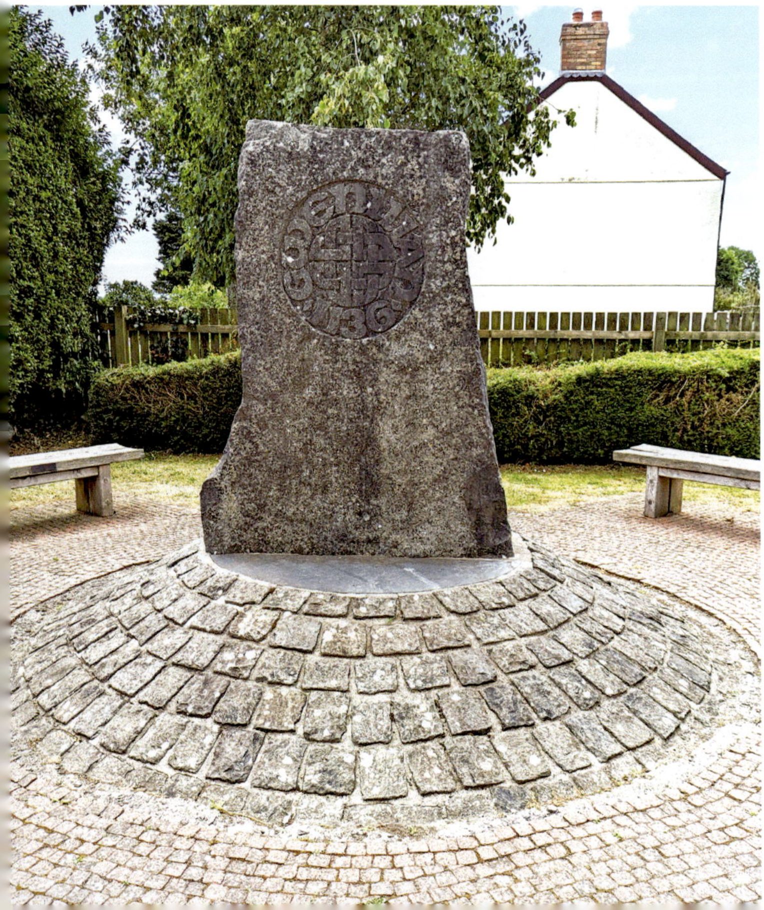

Princess Gwenllian monument.

A fierce battle ensued. Gwenllian was unhorsed, and Morgan was killed attempting to protect her. Gruffydd ap Llewellyn captured Maelgwyn and forced him to watch the bloody capture of his defiant mother. Gwenllian and Maelgwyn were beheaded on the battlefield where they fought for Welsh freedom.

Wellington's Welsh general, Lieutenant General Sir Thomas Picton (1758–1815) had a long association with Carmarthen. He was the highest-ranking officer killed at the Battle of Waterloo (1815), and is the only Welshman buried at St Paul's Cathedral, London.

Hailed by the public of the day as a military genius, hero, and brave soldier, many historians and academics considered Picton Wales's greatest soldier. He was a colourful character, who 'commanded with a voice of twenty trumpets,' described by his commanding officer, Arthur Wellesley, 1st Duke of Wellington, as 'a rough, foul-mouthed devil as ever lived, but he always behaved extremely well'.

Picton joined the army aged thirteen as a cornet (the lowest rank of commissioned officer) and became an excellent soldier who continually impressed his superiors. He achieved many accolades for his gallant bravery, strategic ability, and military successes fighting in the Caribbean and during the Peninsular War (1807–14). After this he was promoted to Lieutenant General.

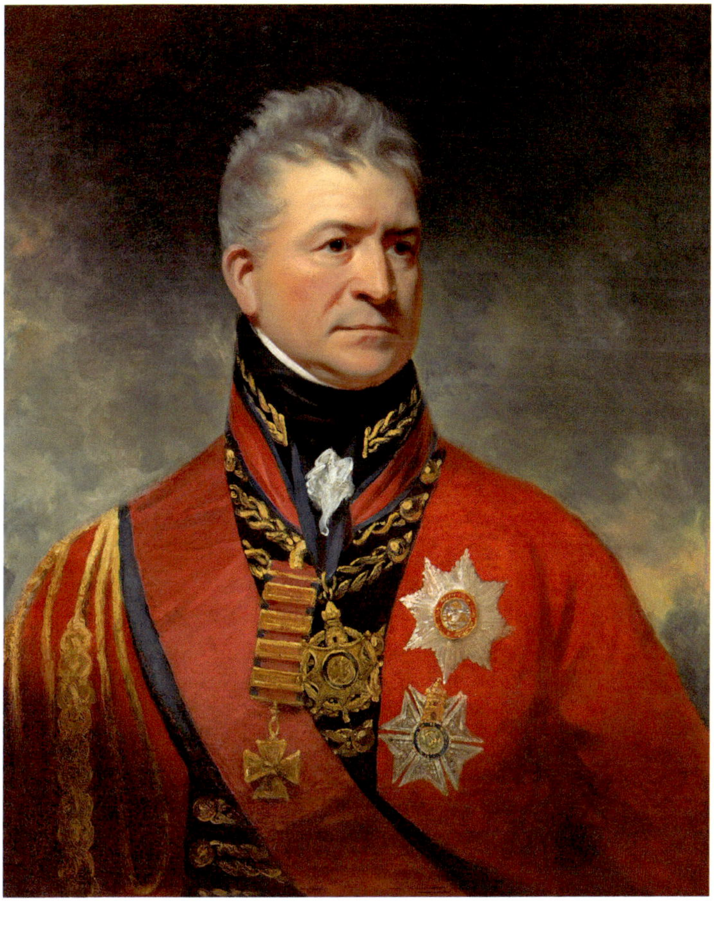

Lieutenant General Sir Thomas Picton. (National Gallery of Art, Washington DC)

During the Battle of Waterloo, when defeat seemed certain, Picton performed his final heroic deed. With two brigades at his command, Picton ordered General Sir Denis's brigade to close a gap in the British line where the French were bursting through. Outnumbering the British four to one, they quickly engulfed the brigade. Defeat seemed imminent.

Realising the danger, Picton galloped to the head of the remaining brigade under the command of General Sir James Kempt. Brandishing his sword, he bellowed, 'Charge! Charge!' Kempt's troops cheered thunderously and, with bayonets fixed, surged to engage the enemy. It was a breathtaking counterattack against overwhelming odds. Picton uttered his last words 'Rally the Highlanders' before he and Kempt's troops plunged into the French forces. Picton was killed when a bullet smashed into his head. His gallant leadership stopped the French in their tracks, enabling the gap to be closed, just when a French victory seemed certain.

His body was repatriated and entombed in the family vault, London. When the vault fell into disrepair, revealing Picton's coffin, Queen Victoria allowed the removal of his body to St Paul's Cathedral in June 1859, where it remains today.

More recently a figure of notoriety, his military prowess has been eclipsed by his exploits as Governor of Trinidad (1797–1803) where his treatment of enslaved and free peoples earned him the nicknames 'Tyrant of Trinidad' and 'Blood-Stained Governor.'

Carmarthenshire is the last resting place of many rank-and-file heroes from great military campaigns, most lost to history. Sergeant John Samuel and Private David Thomas are two such men.

Samuel, Carmarthen's last surviving Peninsular War and Waterloo veteran, was an unsung comrade-in-arms of Lieutenant General Sir Thomas Picton. They fought together in the Peninsular War, at the Battles of Salamanca and Vitoria, and at the sieges of Badajoz and San Sebastian, where Samuel was shot twice in the chest.

He later joined Picton at Waterloo, where early in the battle at Quatre Bras, while performing the dangerous role of letter orderly, a musket ball shattered his right knee. He crawled into a churchyard, dressed his wound, and remained hidden overnight in the freezing rain. The following day, using improvised crutches, he made his way back to Waterloo with his communications before being taken to Brussels for medical treatment.

Samuel joined the Carmarthenshire Fusiliers in 1807 when he was fifteen and enlisted in the Scottish 1st Regiment of Foot in 1811. After Waterloo, he served another eighteen years before retiring in 1833, and returned home to Carmarthen a hero.

When he died aged eighty-eight, Samuel was buried with full military honours at St David's, Carmarthen, the church where he had served as an assistant churchwarden for thirty years. A huge funeral procession followed his coffin from Waun Dew (Richmond Terrace) under militia standards, to the beat of muffled drums, as it snaked along Dark Gate and Lammas Street to the church. In 1977, his headstone along with others was moved to the perimeter wall, where it now rests.

Carmarthen-born David Thomas was a big man, way above the average height of the day (5 feet 4 inches) and was the town's last surviving hero of Balaklava. In 1843, aged twenty-one, he joined the 4th Light Dragoon Guards, billeted in the Penlan workhouse, where earlier that year they had bayonet charged a mob of Rebecca rioters besieging the workhouse.

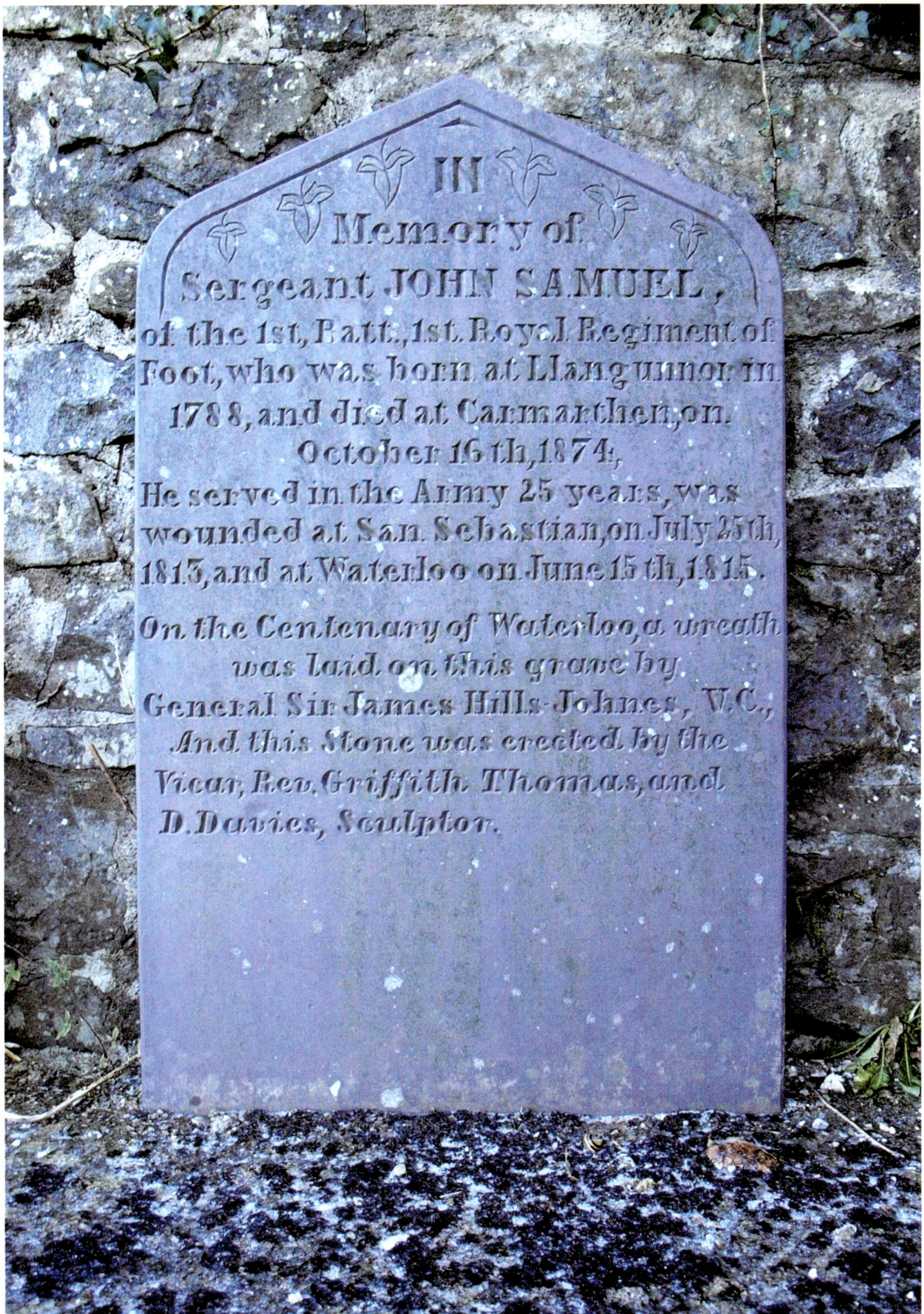

Samuel's headstone.

In 1854, Thomas and his regiment were in the Crimea, part of the Light Brigade of Cavalry, under the command of the Earl of Cardigan. On 25 October, Thomas, along with 600 other cavalry men, drew his sabre to face a heavily defended Russian position along a valley at Balaklava. Cardigan gave the order to advance, and the men rode off into what infamously has become known as the 'Charge of the Light Brigade', Britain's most disastrous cavalry charge.

Having launched their assault, the Light Brigade charged through a crossfire of heavy cannon fire into the smoke and flames of the Russian guns. By the end of the action, only 200 men, over half of whom were wounded, had survived. Thomas bravely fought through the Russian lines and picked up one of his gravely injured officers, carrying him under heavy enemy fire back to British lines.

While his act of valour went unrecognised by a medal, it was remembered by the officer, who, until his death many years later, sent Thomas money during his retirement to Carmarthen. When that money stopped, Thomas was forced to seek refuge in the Penlan Workhouse, where he lived in poverty until his death aged sixty-eight in 1890.

Although Thomas was buried with full military honours at St David's Church, it wasn't until his death that the town realised it had lost another hero. A collection could not raise the full cost of the funeral, six shillings short, and the missing money was eventually made good by a reluctant relative.

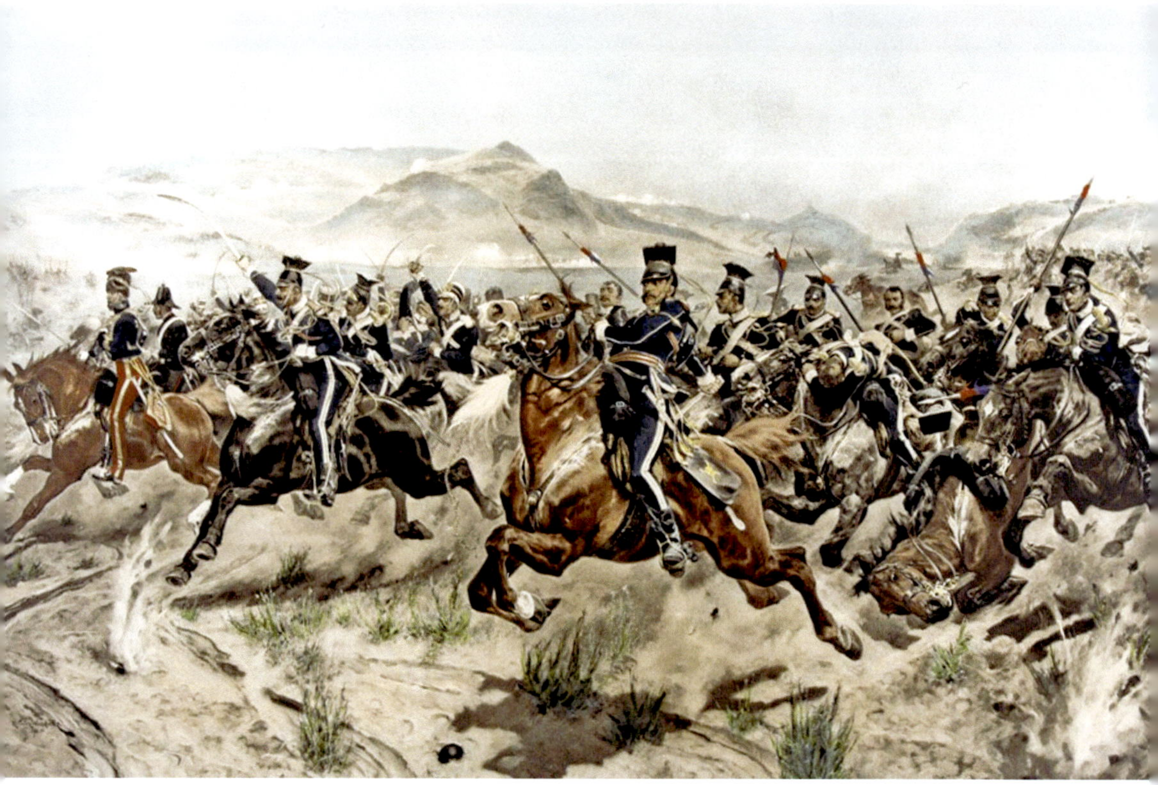

Charge of the Light Brigade. Richard Caton Woodville Jr.

Wales highest scoring 'ace' of the First World War, James Ira Thomas Jones, was born on 18 April 1896 at Woolstone Farm, near St Clears. He enlisted with the 4th Battalion (Territorial) Welsh Regiment in 1913 and when the First World War started he joined the Royal Flying Corps as a first-class air mechanic, wireless section.

Posted to France six months later in July 1915, he began flying combat missions as an observer/gunner. In May 1916, he was on the front line at a wireless interception station when he risked his life rescuing two wounded gunners while under enemy fire. For this he was awarded the Military Medal (MM).

After receiving several commendations for bravery, Jones was awarded the Russian Order of the Cross of St George in January 1917. In May of the same year, he returned to England to begin pilot training. Commissioned in August 1917, he joined No. 74 Squadron and returned to the front line. The Distinguished Flying Cross (DFC) was awarded to him on 3 August 1918 for displaying great courage, skill and initiative while attacking and destroying six enemy aeroplanes in just eleven days.

The Military Cross (MC) came in the following month for his display of conspicuous gallantry and devotion to duty when he engaged and shot down an enemy two-seater aircraft. Ten days later, during a five-day period, he destroyed five enemy aircraft and a balloon before chasing off another aircraft and killing the observer. A second DFC for gallantry as an officer was awarded for destroying twenty-one enemy aeroplanes in a three-month period. In November 1918, he was awarded the Distinguished Service Order (DSO). His citation read: 'Since joining his present brigade in May last, this officer has destroyed twenty-eight enemy machines. He combines skilful tactics and marksmanship with high courage. While engaged on wireless interception duty, he followed a patrol

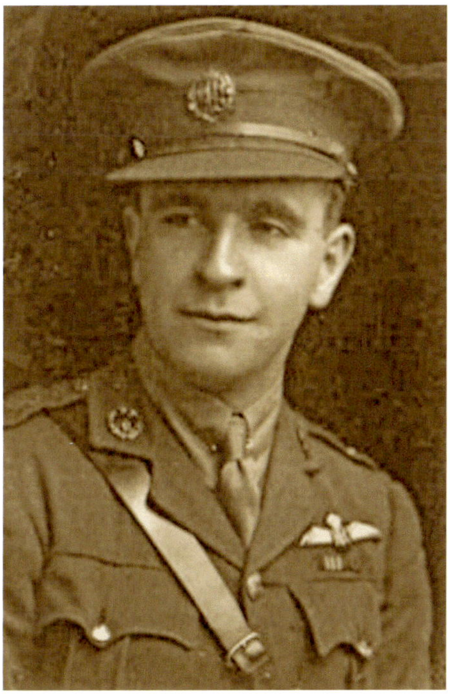

James Ira Thomas Jones.
(www.theaerodrome.com)

of nine Fokker biplanes and succeeded in joining their formation unobserved. After a while two Fokkers left the formation to attack one of our artillery observation machines. Following them, Captain Jones engaged the higher of the two, which fell on its companion, and both machines fell interlocked in flames.'

By the end of the war Jones had become an Air Ace, achieving thirty-seven victories and surviving twenty-eight flight accidents. He continued to serve with the Royal Air Force (RAF), retiring on 9 July 1936 at the rank of Wing Commander.

War with Germany was imminent, and Jones was recalled to the RAF in August 1939. Amazingly, he topped his First World War achievements with his most daring act of bravery yet. In July 1940, flying an unarmed Hawker Henley light bomber, he spotted a German Junkers Ju 88 bomber near Swansea, pursued it, and attacked it with his flare gun. This action caused the Junkers to break off their attack. He survived the war, dying on 30 August 1960, following a fall at his home in Aberaeron. He is buried at Cana Chapel Cemetery, near Bancyfelin, Carmarthen.

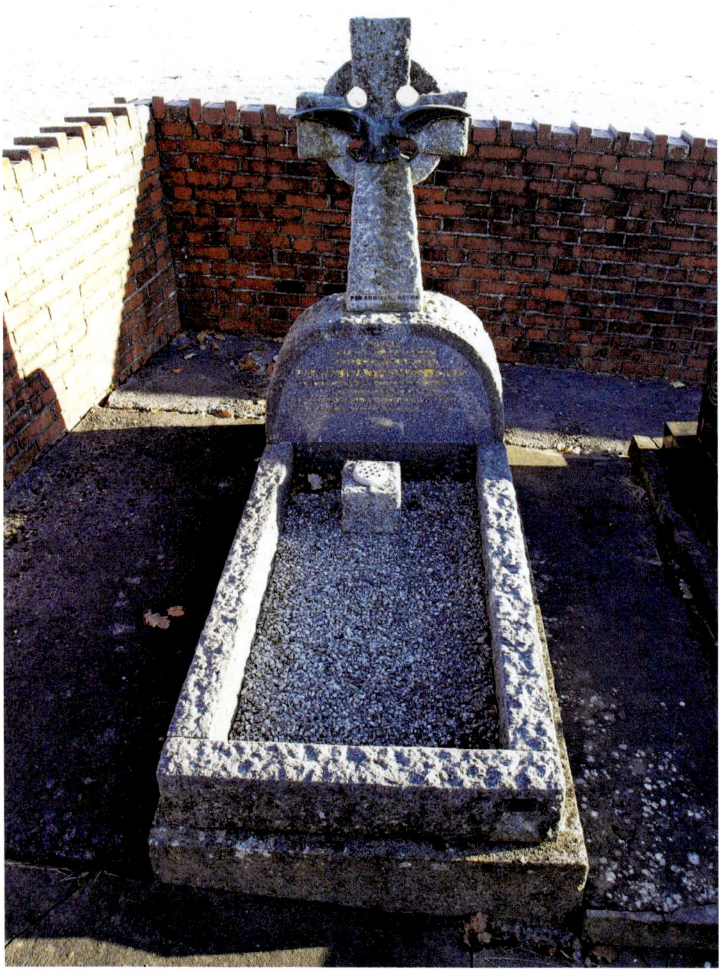

Grave of James Ira Thomas Jones.

Raymond Hiley Harries was born in Llandilofawr, Carmarthenshire, in 1916. When war broke out, in 1939 he joined the Royal Air Force Volunteer Reserve (RAFVR) as an airman. In 1942, having completed pilot training, he joined No. 131 Squadron at Llanbedr, Gwynedd, as a flight commander. He spared no effort in training his pilots and fostered a fine team spirit. During numerous sorties he destroyed one and assisted in the destruction of two other enemy aircraft. For this and for also showing outstanding leadership he was awarded a DFC in September 1942.

Harries took part in the aerial operations supporting the Dieppe Raid on 19 August 1942. He claimed one kill and shared in two others. In May 1943, he was awarded a second DFC for destroying three enemy aircraft, assisting in the destruction of another, and damaging three more. He was a highly efficient squadron commander who, through his great keenness and energetic leadership, set a tremendous example.

While in command of No. 91 Squadron at Hawkinge, Kent, Harries became the highest scoring Griffon Spitfire ace with eleven kills, and was given credit for downing a V-1 flying bomb. In September 1943, he received a third DFC for being a fine leader, a skilful and tenacious fighter pilot and for destroying a further four enemy aircraft.

Later that year Harries was awarded the Distinguished Service Order (DSO), for being an exceptionally skilful, courageous, and determined fighter pilot, who during October led his force on various sorties, shooting down twenty-seven enemy aircraft, three of them by his guns.

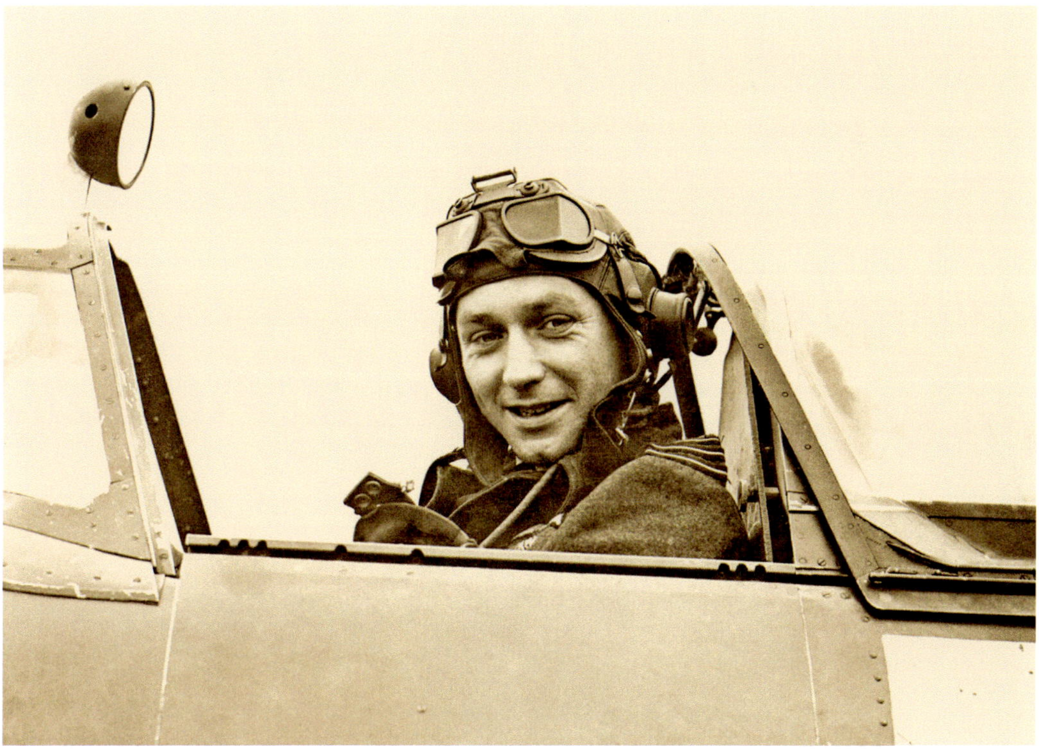

Raymond Hiley Harries (Royal Air Force official photographer).

The Free French Airforce awarded Harries the Croix de Guerre (France) and the Croix de Guerre (Belgium) in March 1944. Incredibly, he received a second DSO in 1945. No citation exists outlining what act(s) of courage he performed to merit it.

Harries died on 14 May 1950 flying a Gloster Meteor F4, which ran out of fuel and stalled. He attempted to bale out, but his parachute got tangled in the rear wing, and he was killed. He is buried in All Saints churchyard, Newton-on-Ouse, North Yorkshire.

The Victoria Cross (VC) is the highest and most prestigious award of the British honours system and awarded for valour 'in the presence of the enemy' to members of the British armed forces. Carmarthenshire has three connections with recipients.

During an impeccable military career James Hills-Johnes (1833–1919) rose through the ranks to Lieutenant General. He saw active service in the Indian Mutiny (1857), Abyssinian Expedition (1867), Lushai Expedition (1871–72), and Second Anglo-Afghan War (1878–1880).

As a twenty-three-year-old second lieutenant in the Bengal Horse Artillery during the Indian Mutiny he was awarded the VC for 'displaying very gallant conduct in defending the position assigned to him in case of alarm' at the Siege of Delhi, 9 July 1857. He was also mentioned in dispatches for bravery four times. He became the High Sheriff of Carmarthenshire in 1886, was made a Knight Grand Cross of the Order of the Bath (GCB) in June 1893. and was an honorary freeman of Carmarthen in 1910. He died of influenza on 3 January 1919, aged eighty-five, and is buried at St Cynwyl's Church, Caio.

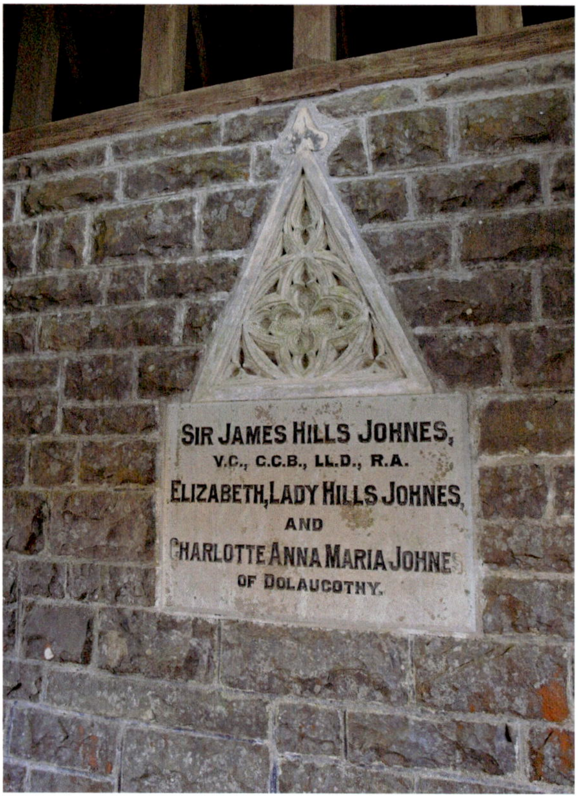

Lychgate, Cynwyl Church.

Jacob Thomas (1833–1911) was born in Llanwinio, Carmarthenshire. He was a bombardier in the Bengal Artillery during the Indian Mutiny and awarded a VC for displaying distinguished gallantry on 27 September 1857 at the Siege of Lucknow.

Jacob, part of a mixed detachment of infantry and artillerymen from the 32nd Regiment of Foot and Madras Fusiliers, arrived in the city to destroy and capture guns. Several gunners became disorientated and lost in the narrow lanes leading towards an enemy battery. The detachment reached the guns but had to wait for the gunners to arrive to destroy the guns.

To destroy the guns powder was rammed down the barrel and the muzzle blocked with clay. Unfortunately, because the day was so hot, the soldiers had drunk all their water and the clay was too dry. The detachment had to abandon the guns and make its way back to their camp outside the city.

Rebels lined their escape route, causing the British soldiers to run a gauntlet of musket fire, and they sustained several casualties. One of them was a collapsed Fusilier. Thomas picked him up and carried him over his shoulder to the safety of a barricade under constant enemy fire. For this heroic act, Thomas was awarded the VC. On his retirement, he lived and then died in India aged seventy-seven.

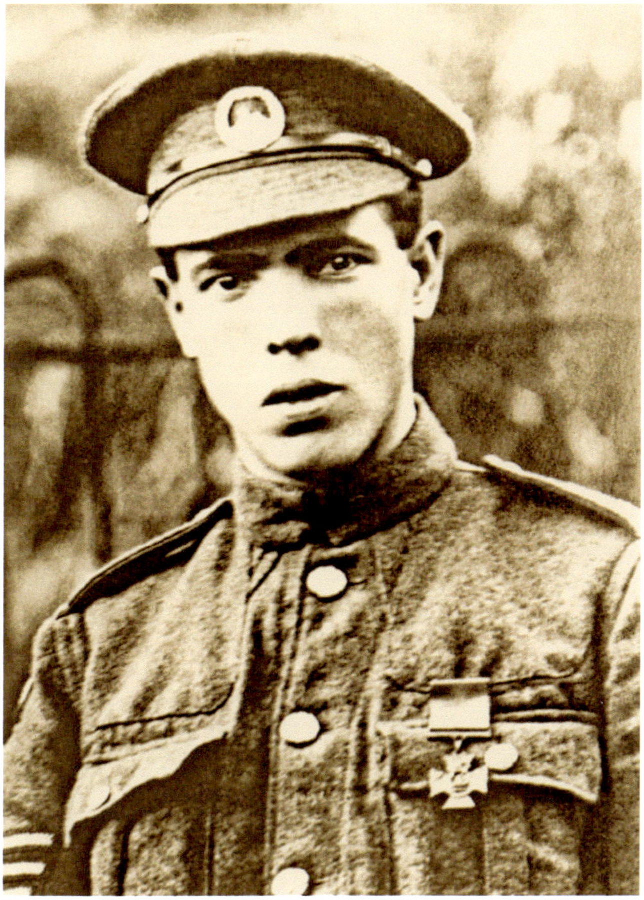

Ivor Rees.

Ivor Rees (1893–1967) was born in Felinfoel, near Llanelli, Carmarthenshire. When war broke at in 1914, he enlisted into the 11th Battalion, South Wales Borderers, part of the 115th Brigade, 38th (Welsh) Division. In July 1916 having survived fierce fighting at Mametz Wood, during the Somme offensive, the division moved to Ypres. The battalion's job during the Battle of Passchendaele (31 July–10 November 1917) was to capture the Pilckem Ridge, a heavily fortified German defensive line.

For his actions during the attack, Rees, now a sergeant, was awarded the VC. His citation reads: 'At Pilckem, Belgium, on 31st July 1917, an enemy machine gun inflicted many casualties when it opened fire at close range. Sergeant Rees, leading his platoon, gradually worked his way round the right flank, by making short rushes to the rear of the gun position. At 20 yards from the machine gun, Sergeant Rees rushed forward towards it, shooting one of the crew, and bayoneting the other. He bombed a large concrete emplacement, killing five of the enemy and taking 30 prisoners, including two officers, and capturing a machine gun, undamaged.'

At Llanelli Town Hall, a blue plaque commemorates Ivor Rees being awarded the Victoria Cross.

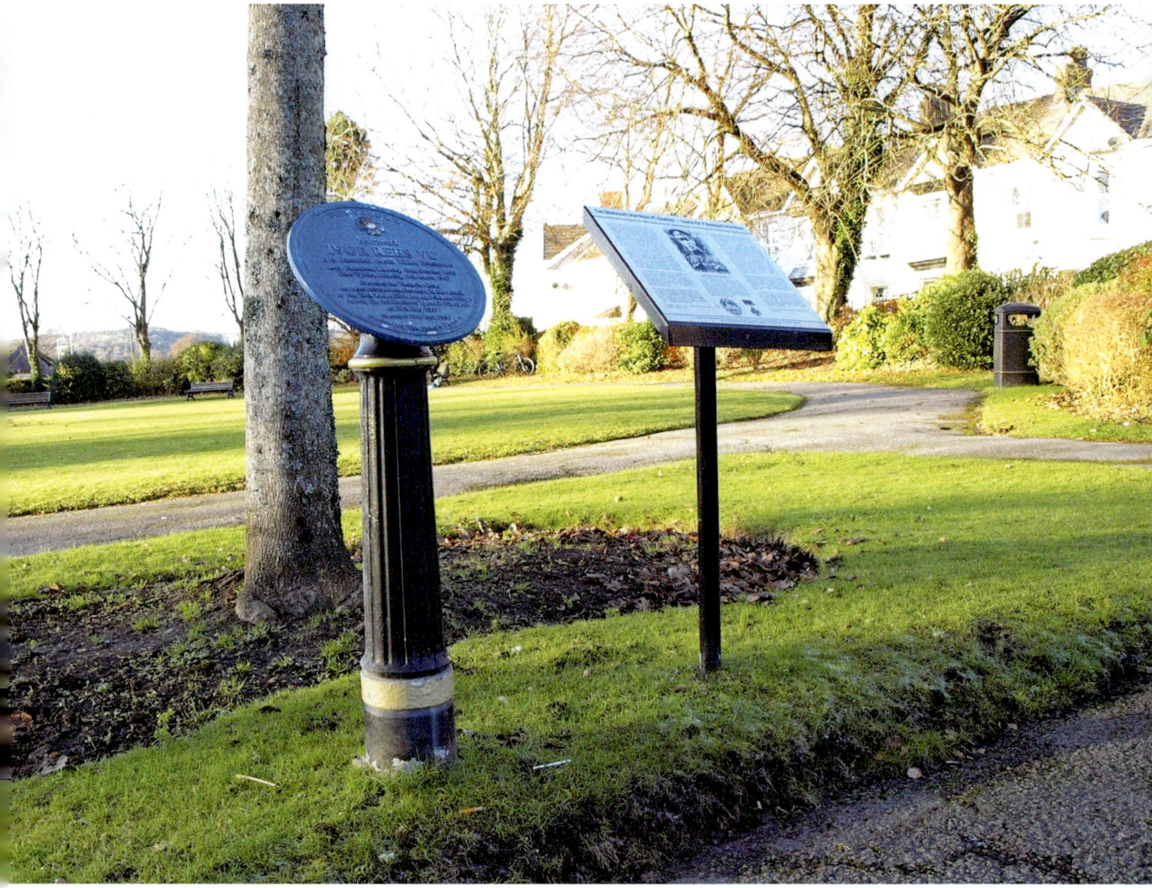

Ivor Rees plaque.

7

Munitions and Explosives

Pembrey Country Park was once home to a labyrinth of hidden tunnels and bunkers known as Pembrey Munitions Factory. The large sand dunes offered substantial protection in the event of an explosion, making it the perfect location for a munitions factory.

The earliest factory was built to produce gunpowder and comprised eighty small sheds serviced by a narrow-gauge railway. It was constructed in 1881 across 150 acres of land that included the old harbour and docks.

The first explosives, detonators, and fuses for industrial use in collieries and quarries were manufactured there by the New Explosives Company Limited. In late October 1882, it became the first successful commercial manufacturers of guncotton (a replacement for gunpowder as a propellant in firearms) in Britain.

On 11 November 1882, a minor explosion occurred. A week later on 17 November a devastating blast killed seven workers aged thirteen to twenty-four. The blast was heard in Tenby and rattled windows in Burry Port.

Despite introducing enhanced security features, the incident bankrupted the New Explosives Company Limited, and they were replaced on 22 May 1885 by a subsidiary of the Nobel's Explosives Company Ltd, the South Wales Explosive Company. While manufacturing explosives had stopped on the site, it continued to store and distribute dynamite until 13 May 1893, when a fire destroyed three large storage sheds.

The Nobel's Explosives Company Ltd redeveloped the site and by 1914 it was producing industrial explosives. When Britain entered the First World War in August 1914, Lord Kitchener, Secretary of State for War, contracted Nobel's Explosives to construct and manage a purpose-built munitions factory at Pembrey to support the war effort.

Preparing the ground and erecting sheds began during the winter of 1914 and by May 1915, around 1,800 people were employed in munitions work in two adjacent factories. Most of the young men were on active service with the armed forces or engaged in wartime occupations like coal mining, agriculture, railways, or construction, so most of the munition's workers were women. Later that month, the larger factory began producing TNT, a powerful explosive used in bombs, shells, depth charges and naval mines, along with the less powerful explosive cordite, which replaced gunpowder as a propellant for military weapon systems.

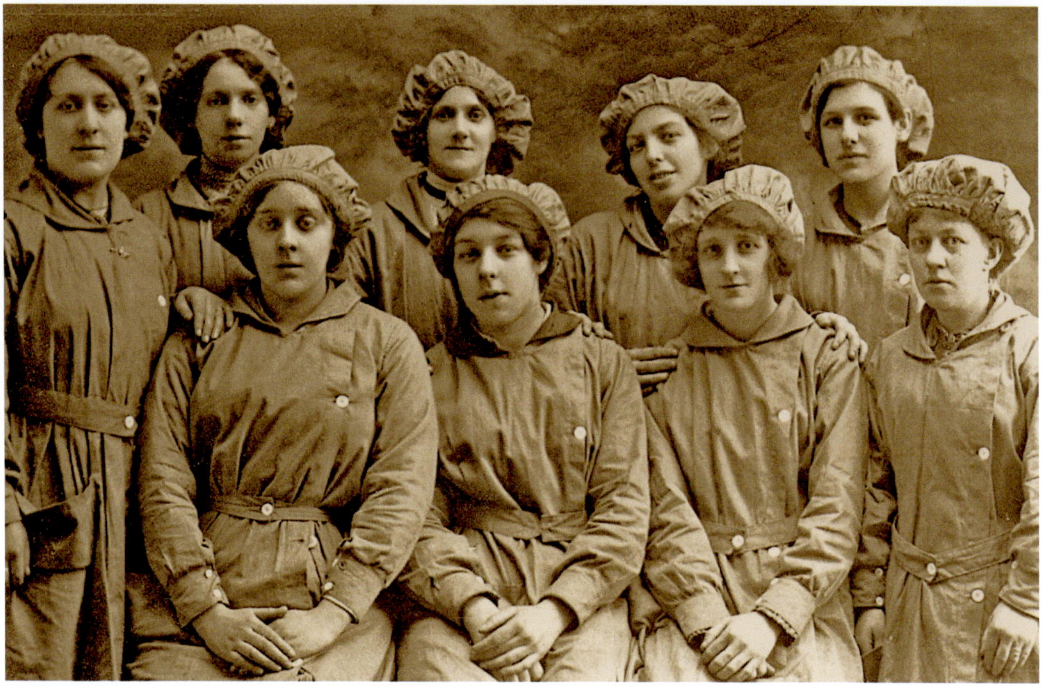

Munitions workers, *c.* 1916.

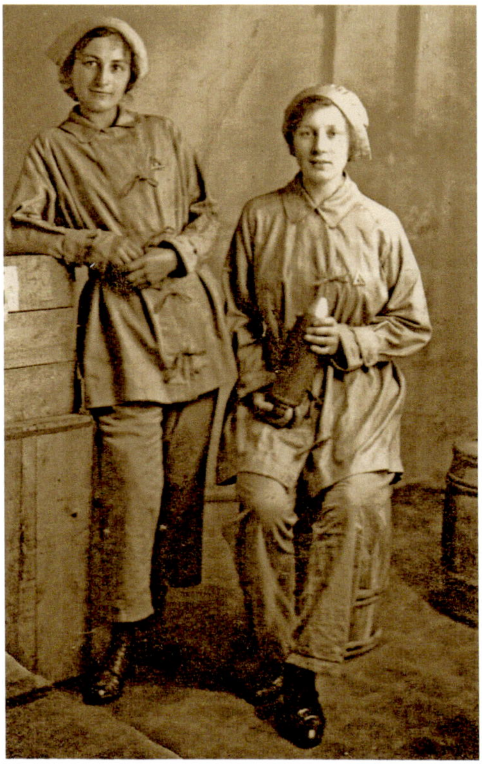

Munitions workers, *c.* 1916.

A second separate loading factory, the National Filling Factory No. 18, was built that same month by the Explosives Loading Company. This was equipped to fill shells for the Admiralties mines, torpedoes and other explosive ordnance, with TNT and cordite manufactured at the larger factory.

During 1916, the factory began producing cordite paste, rifle cordite, ballistite and ordnance cordite. Then on the 1 January 1917, the Ministry of Munitions, a body created to co-ordinate the production and distribution of munitions for the war effort, nationalised both factories, renaming them HM Explosive Factory No. 126.

On 14 July, only six months later, an unexplained explosion killed six people, and on 18 November 1918 three workers died in another explosion while disassembling an eighteen-pound high explosive shell.

Employees travelled extensively to work at the factory. They completed fifty-six hours per week at sixpence an hour, plus a weekly war bonus of three shillings and sixpence. By 1918 the site employed 4,765 workers, 60 per cent of whom were female.

A special train station for factory workers was created on the GWR main line at Pembrey, and special trains ran from Llanelli, Carmarthen, and Swansea to transport employees directly to the factory. This invasion of workers led to chronic housing problems. News reports of serious increases in drunkenness and inappropriate behaviour abounded in the local area.

Munitions production work was hard, repetitive, and undertaken in hazardous conditions. Women were given milk to drink to combat the effects of these dangerous compounds, but personal protective clothing dealt inadequately with fumes from chemical

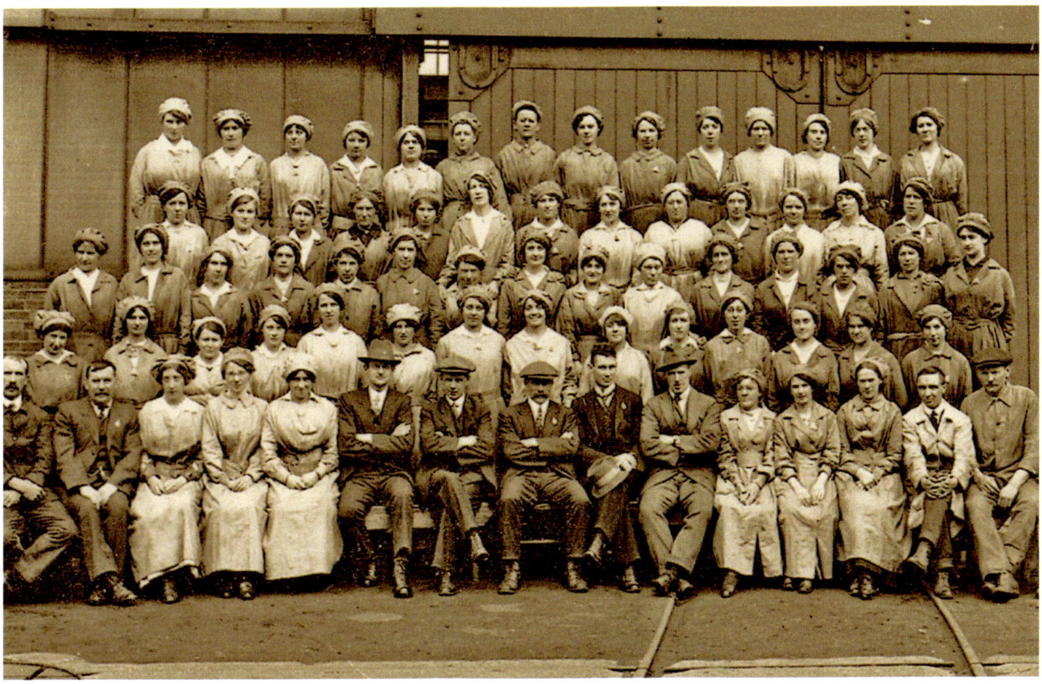

Munitions workers, *c.* 1916.

solutions. Many employees suffered eye and lung problems. Thirty women per shift suffered epileptic fits per day, and in the acid section airborne acid particles rotted clothes, impaired breathing, and prickled skin.

Women working with TNT and cordite were affectionately nicknamed 'Canary Girls' because the TNT caused a toxic jaundice that turned their hair ginger, skin, and nails yellow, and caused their teeth to break or fall out. Some women became blind, others lost fingers and hands from burns.

Turning yellow was not the only health risk. The only way of filling shell cases was by hand. Employees would take the casing and use a scoop to fill it with 'the devil's porridge', a toxic powder mixture through the top opening. They would then compact the powder down before placing a detonator on top, which was also tapped down. Tapping too hard would cause the shell to explode. Side effects from inhaling contaminated dust and noxious fumes included headaches, hysteria, fits, nausea, hives, liver toxicity, anaemia, and blindness. They proved fatal for some workers.

Requests for masks were denied on the grounds they caused dermatitis. This allowed prolonged exposure to TNT, causing liver failure, anaemia, and spleen enlargement. In the canteen, these women were separated from other employees because everything they

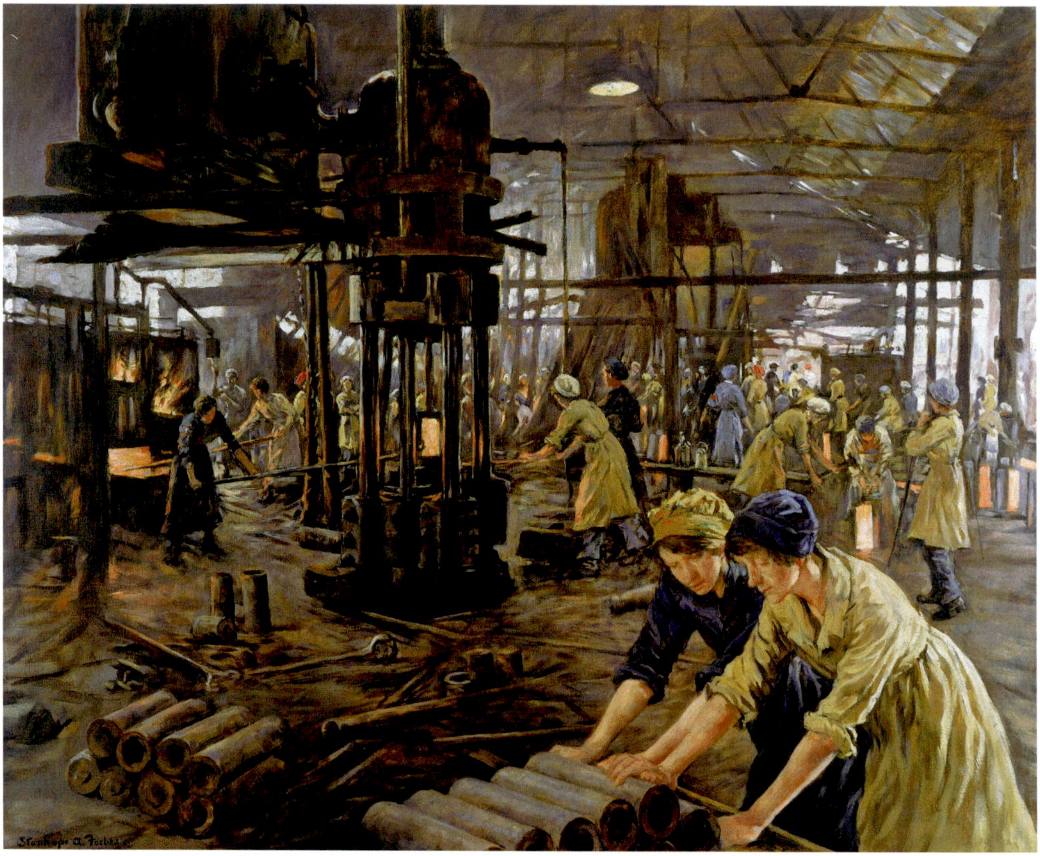

Stanhope Forbes. (Wellcome Collection)

touched turned yellow. Despite segregation and changes in skin and hair colour, many workers regarded it as a badge of honour, showing they were doing dangerous war work. At its peak, the Filling Factory produced over 200 tons of high explosives shells every week and in less than two years, it had exported 1,143,000 shells to Europe and the Middle East. By the end of the war the site occupied 771 acres. The factories, site buildings, and cottages were completely self-contained with their own; boiler houses, power stations, pumping plants, a weighbridge, 13 and half miles of railway track, sidings, and 21 and a half miles of tramways, plus a 100-circuit automatic telephonic system. Four million gallons of water was consumed daily, piped from the Gwendraeth Fawr and Fach, to an underground reservoir on the site where it was treated and stored in tanks.

Shell filling ceased in May 1917, and by the end of the year, only 1,050 workers remained in the factory. Seventy per cent were female. By the end of 1919, with the war over, the site ceased production and during the early 1920s it was sold to a local firm of breakers and scrap merchants for £30,000.

The factory's general administration offices were not reclaimed but used as a school camp for miners' children from the poorest areas of South Wales, who spent a fortnight there improving their health. In April 1938 as war in Europe once again threatened, the War Office acquired the site of the school camp for defence purposes, causing it to close in June that year.

Later that year the Ministry of Supply commissioned a new factory on 500 acres of the former Nobel's Explosives Company site at Pembrey. The Royal Ordnance Factory (ROF) No. 54 one of eight ROF in Wales was completed during 1939. Many of the earlier manufacturing buildings were demolished, but the pumphouse and administration building survived.

With the world once again at war, the production of TNT began in December 1939. The ROF was one of four munitions factories producing TNT in the UK. Workers could earn up to £3 for a forty-five-hour week, with meals and transport costs included. By comparison, the Women's Land Army pay was £1 and eight shillings for a fifty-hour week, half of which was given to the farmer for food and accommodation. The disruption to family and social life by the factory's shift system created a strong camaraderie amongst the workforce which more than compensated for any inconvenience. People wanted to do their bit for the war effort, and the dangers of munitions work were accepted as part of that effort.

At its height, the factory employed 3,000 workers, becoming the UK's largest supplier of TNT. The factory also produced ammonium nitrate, combined with TNT to create the explosive amatol.

The factory was a major target for German bombers during the war years. Pilots from nearby RAF Pembrey's fighter squadrons prevented most enemy sorties from reaching there. On 10 July 1940 at 12.20 a daylight raid by a single German bomber, guided by unconcealed roads, dropped ten 110-pound high explosive bombs and wreaked havoc on the factory. The first bomb fell near the entrance gates, and by the end of the attack several production buildings were damaged along with a mains water supply and electricity transformer. The attack was brief but deadly, claiming the lives of ten people and seriously injuring fifteen others. Most of the fatalities occurred in the main dining hall.

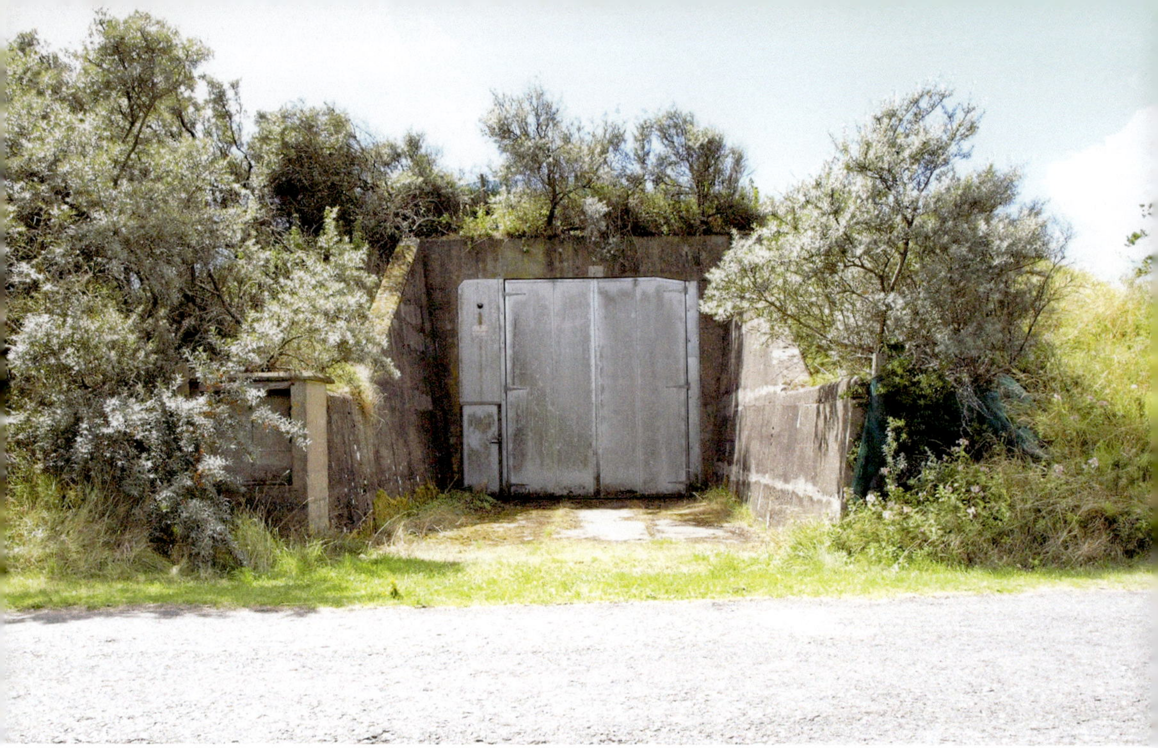

Munitions bunker.

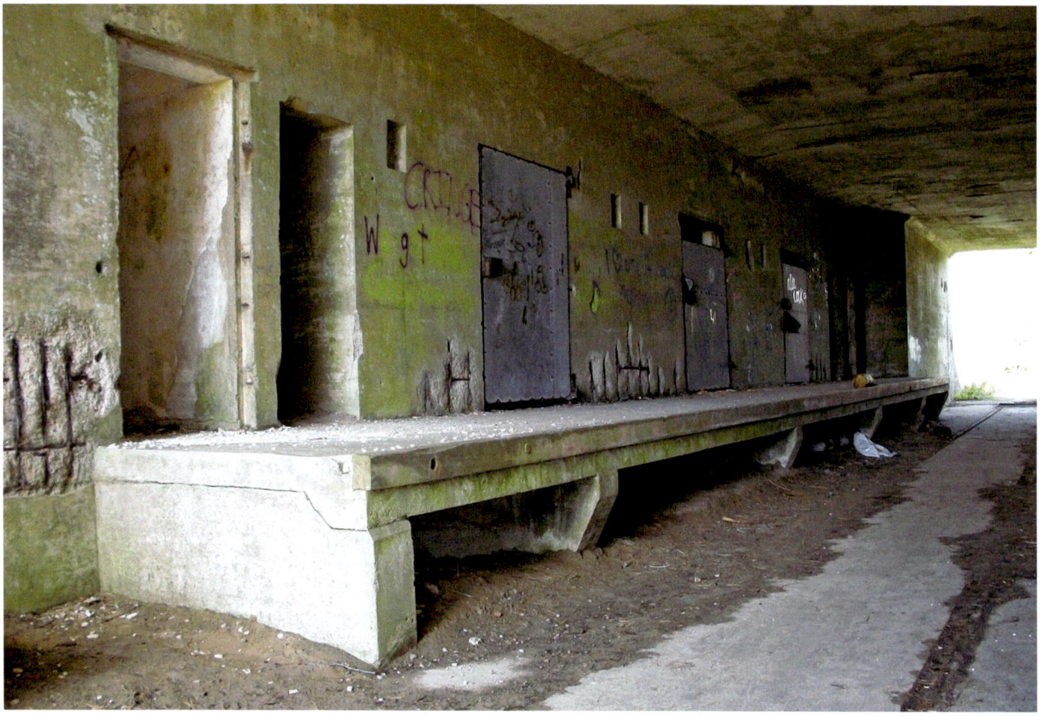

Munitions bunker.

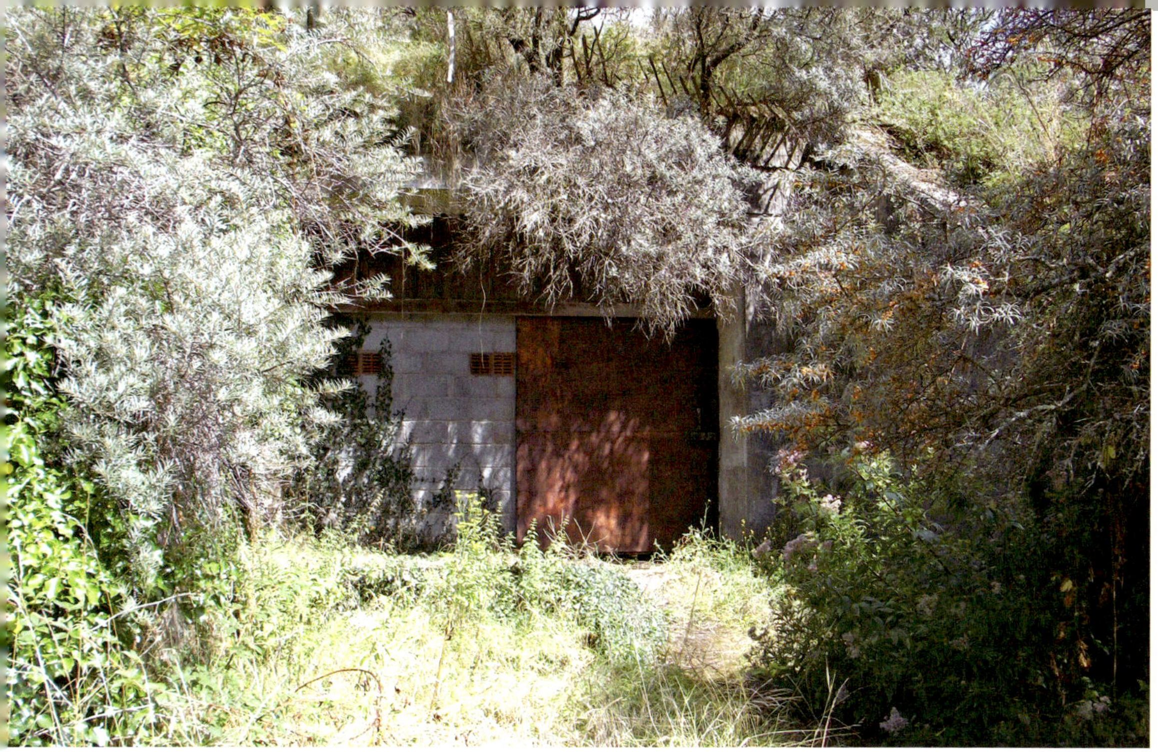

Munitions bunker.

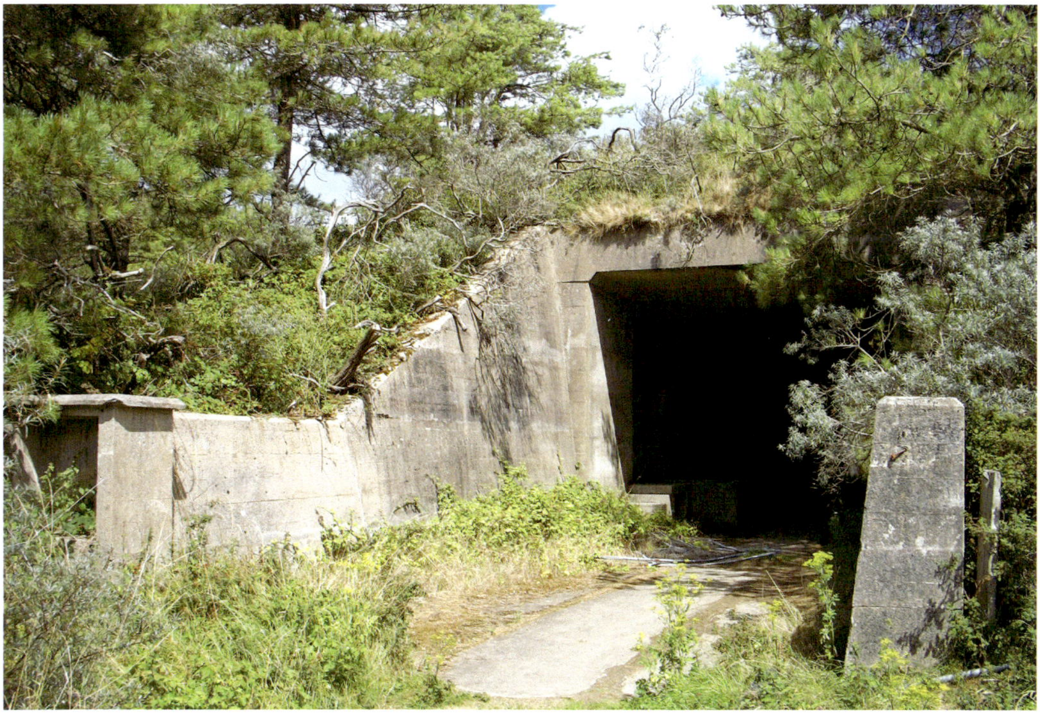

Munitions bunker.

The dead and injured were taken to hospitals by ambulances and private cars. Despite the damage, production returned to full capacity within forty-eight hours. It was important not to let the enemy know how successful their raids had been and wartime censorship makes it difficult to establish the true number of casualties. Further casualties occurred the following year on the 1 November 1941, when two more workers were killed in an explosion at the site's mono-nitration plant. Munitions wages were comparatively good.

In 1944, the factory started breaking down defective ammunition to extract TNT, which was then burnt off, creating 'carbon black', which was harvested for printer's ink. After the war, demand for munitions dwindled, and the ROF continued breaking down surplus ammunition.

It will never be known for certain how many accidents or deaths occurred at Pembrey during the war years. Details of those that were investigated, or subject to a coroner's inquest or public enquiry were curtailed by national reporting restrictions of the day.

The Korean War (1950–53) saw a slight uplift in production at the ROF, but the steady decline in munitions activity during the ensuing decade saw Pembrey's tasks sent elsewhere. In December 1963, the ROF closed.

Between 1969 and 1970, a local campaign and a public inquiry successfully fought a proposal to move the Shoeburyness experimental gunnery range, Essex, to the Pembrey peninsula. This allowed the site to be cleared, remodelled, and created as a country park opening to the public in 1980.

8

Monuments and Memorials

There is no legal definition of a war memorial, and they take many forms, from private and personal markers to imposing public monuments. They remember people, animals, places, and events. The most abundant memorials commemorate the First World War and Second World War, but many other conflicts are also honoured.

It was not until the end of the nineteenth century that Britain began commemorating its war dead; before then, national memorials were rare and often in local churches, dedicated to individual officers or regiments. The first large-scale commemoration for the rank-and-file soldier came after the Second Boer War (1899–1902) when public donations and subscriptions were used to erect prominent memorials. These ranged from metal plaques and stone tablets to statues and obelisks. The most common are brass plaques like those at St Barnabas' Church, Drefach Felindre, and St Cynog Church, Llangynog.

It is not possible to comment on all the county's memorials in this chapter. However, Stephen John's excellent online site West Wales War Memorial Project, at ww1.Wales. offers a comprehensive list and description of the county's monuments and memorials.

This chapter studies some of the military monuments and memorials commemorating the civilians, military units, men, and women of the county who served or died on active service at home and abroad.

Carmarthenshire's oldest military memorial was built around 1805 on the summit of a hill south-east of Llanarthney village. The monument remembers Admiral Nelson and his victories and is known as Paxton's Tower, after Sir William Paxton, former burgess, mayor of Carmarthen, and Welsh Member of Parliament for Carmarthen.

In 1802, Paxton spent £15,000 to secure votes in the county election and offered to build a free bridge over the Towy if he succeeded. When Paxton lost the election, he used the money for the bridge to build the tower in honour of his friend Nelson. Its location was chosen to remind the electorate of their foolishness in not electing him.

Erected between 1825 and 1828 at the west end of Carmarthen town, an elaborate statue of Lieutenant-General Sir Thomas Picton GCB stands on a 75-feet-high square column. A series of carved reliefs adorned it, including one that showed Picton falling wounded from his horse at Waterloo (1815). Another depicted the Siege of Badajoz (1812) with Picton scaling the walls with his men. The reliefs were built of Roman cement, and within a few

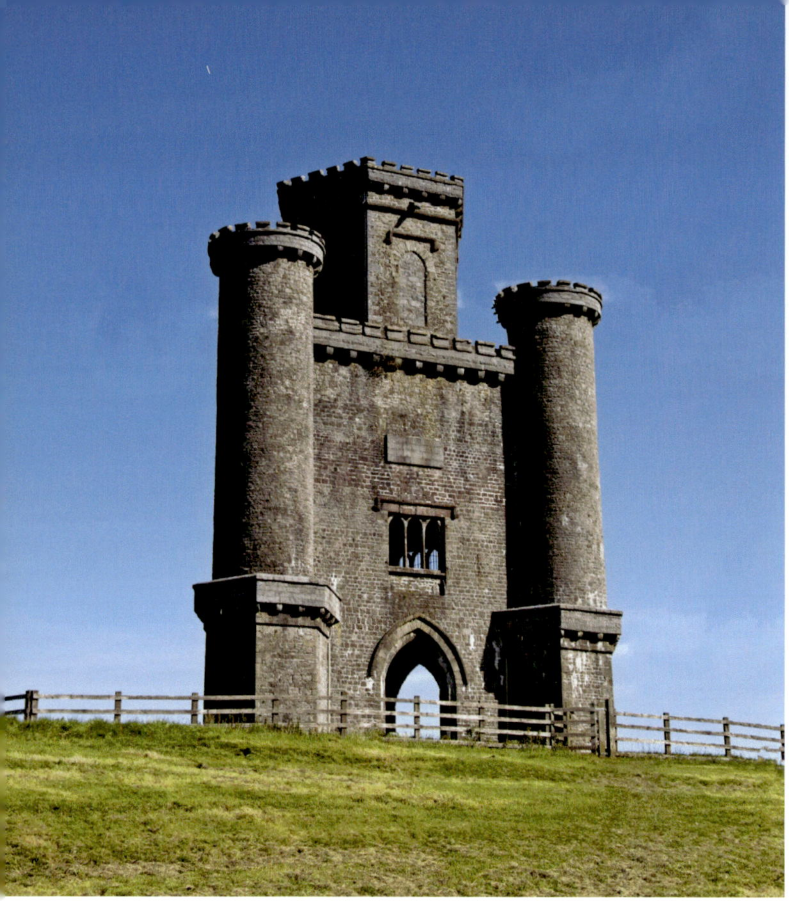

Paxton's Tower (D).

years succumbed to Carmarthen's weather; they were removed in 1846. Replacements were constructed but were never erected. These were rediscovered in Johnstown during the 1970s and are now on display in the Carmarthenshire County Museum.

This monument was replaced in 1888 by the closest thing Wales has to London's Nelson's Column, a plain grey limestone obelisk mounted on a high square pedestal. Originally, the pedestal was intended to carry four lions, but cannons were chosen, though since removed.

The county's next oldest war memorial is a stylish bronze figure of Major-General Sir William Nott standing in the former Market Place of Carmarthen. Created in 1849 from guns captured at the Battle of Maharajpur, India (1843), it was erected in February 1851. Its inauguration was delayed twice, and it remained covered by a large cloak. The *Carmarthen Journal* reported that the statue of General Nott, in its covered state, was a disgrace to the town and an eyesore. It remained thus until 4 o'clock on the morning of 22 October 1851, when a group, referred to as St Peter's boys, climbed over the railings and doused the covering in turpentine, then set fire to it. Witnesses stated the fire blazed so well it alarmed residents who thought a house was aflame.

The scorched statue of Nott was revealed to the townspeople for the first time and has remained viewable since. He is in contemporary dress with a full-length draped mantle falling from his shoulders, his right hand resting on his hip, the left holding the pommel of his sword.

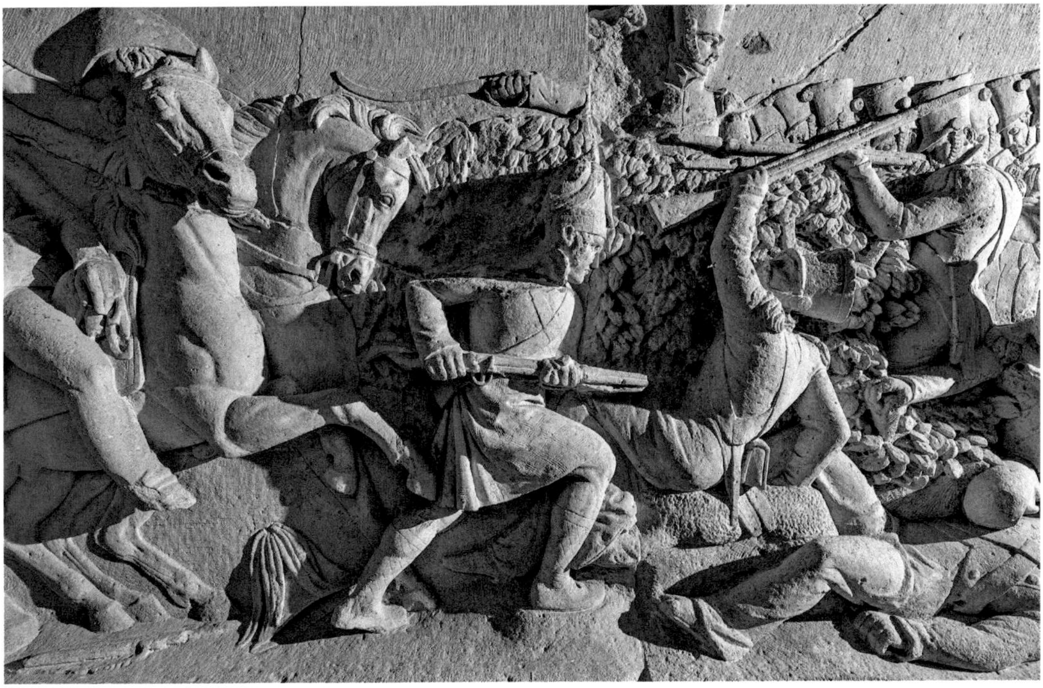

Section of the Picton Freeze. (Courtesy of Carmarthenshire County Museum)

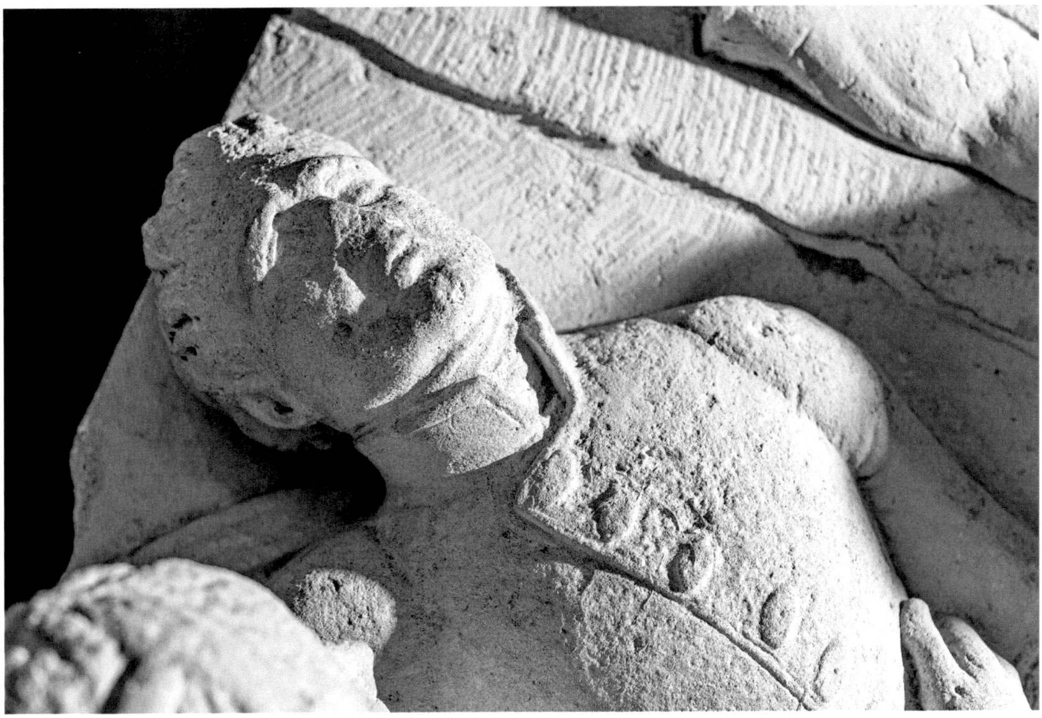

Section of the Picton Freeze. (Courtesy of Carmarthenshire County Museum)

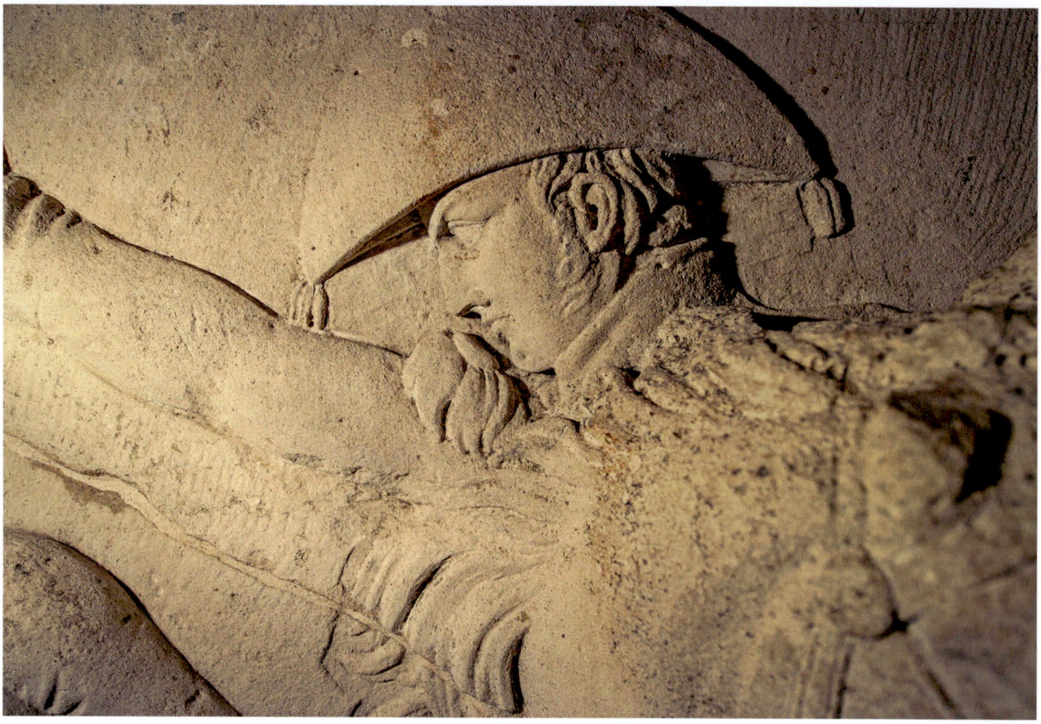

Section of the Picton Freeze. (Courtesy of Carmarthenshire County Museum)

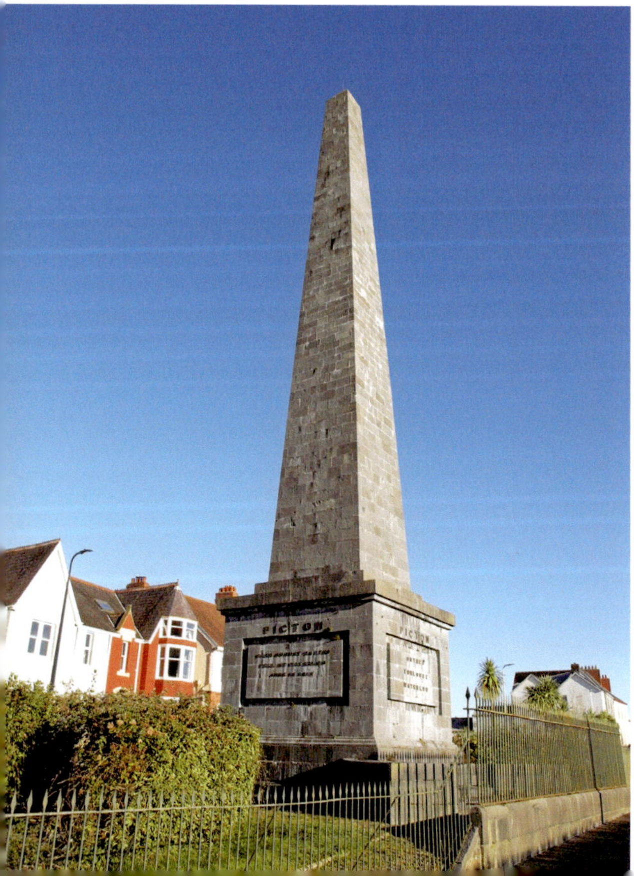

Picton's Obelisk.

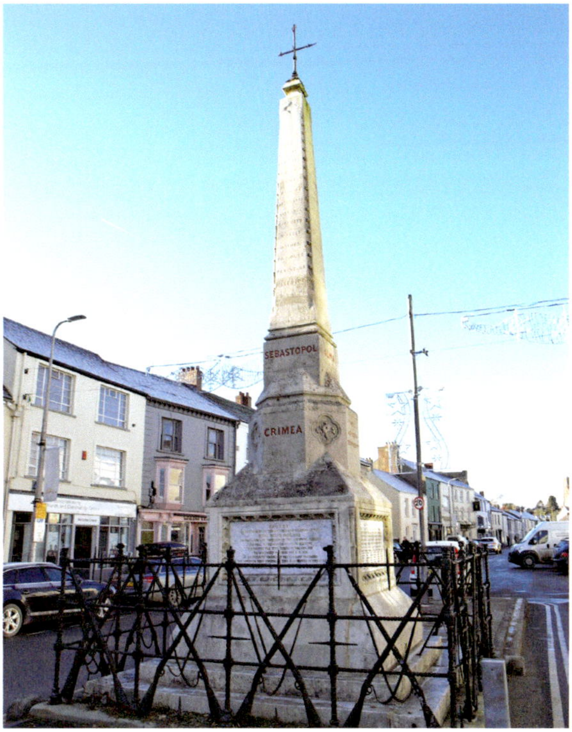

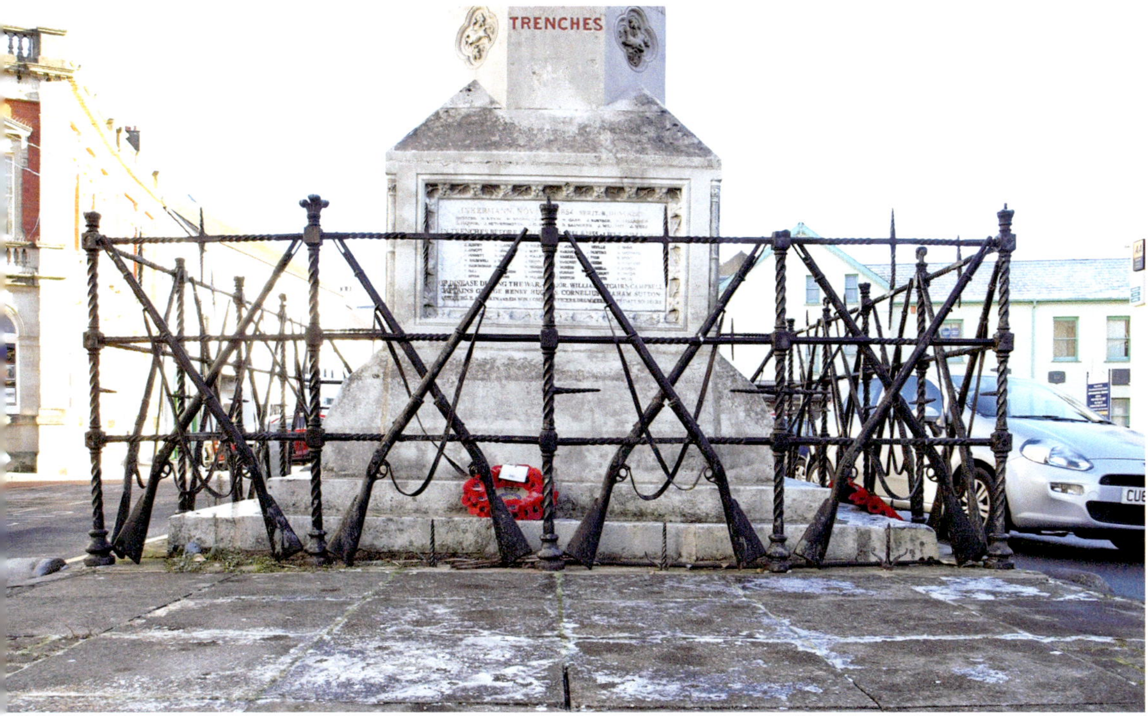

Crimean War Memorial, Carmarthen.

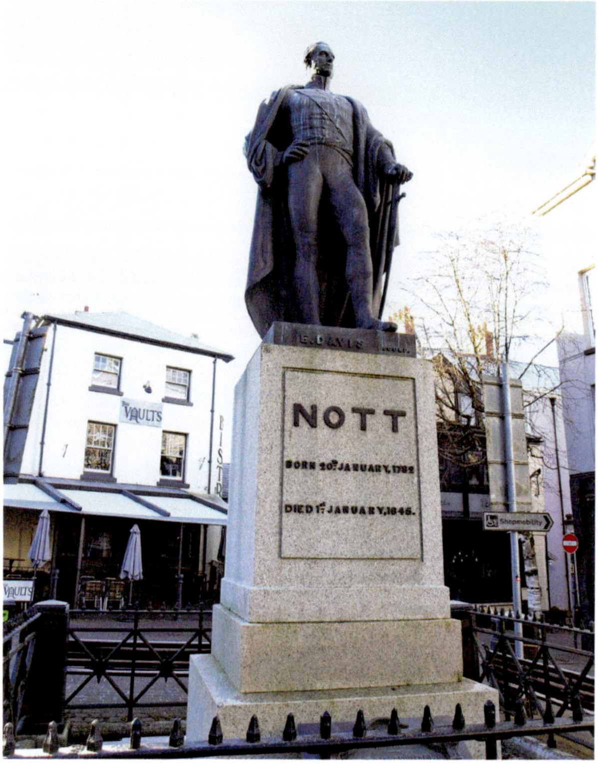

Major-General Sir William Nott.

Another obelisk stands in Lammas Street, Carmarthen. The Gothic-style obelisk, erected in 1858 and made of Portland stone, is uniquely surrounded by iron railings made of crossed muskets with bayonets fixed. It stands upon a square plinth carved with the names Sebastobol, Alma, Redan, and Inkerman, the battles in which men of the 23rd Regiment of Foot, today known as the Royal Welch Fusiliers, fought during the Crimean War (1853–56). The memorial panels are inscribed with the names of 313 officers and soldiers of the Royal Welsh fusiliers who died during the conflict, and 526 unnamed non-commissioned officers, drummers and private soldiers of the regiment.

The monument was erected at the expense of Captain, later General, Sir Daniel Lysons, who led the first British troops, a company of the 23rd, to enter Crimea. A captured Russian gun from the war once stood in front of it but was later removed and is now lost.

While several monuments include memorials to men who died during the South African War (1899–1902). The county has two monuments dedicated to the conflict. The first is a bronze statue of a rifleman, bareheaded with a pith helmet at his feet and standing on a tall grey granite pedestal, in the Town Hall Gardens at Llanelli. Dedicated on the 26 August 1905, it commemorates the lives of nine men from the town and district who died. The statue is a replica of a bronze original that stood in West Hartlepool, County Durham, until it was stolen in March 1968. The other stands in the Guildhall Square, Carmarthen, a stone figure of an officer in Boer War campaign dress and slouch hat standing at ease on a red granite plinth. Unveiled in 1906, the monument honours the memory of thirty-three of the county's 'sons' who died during the war.

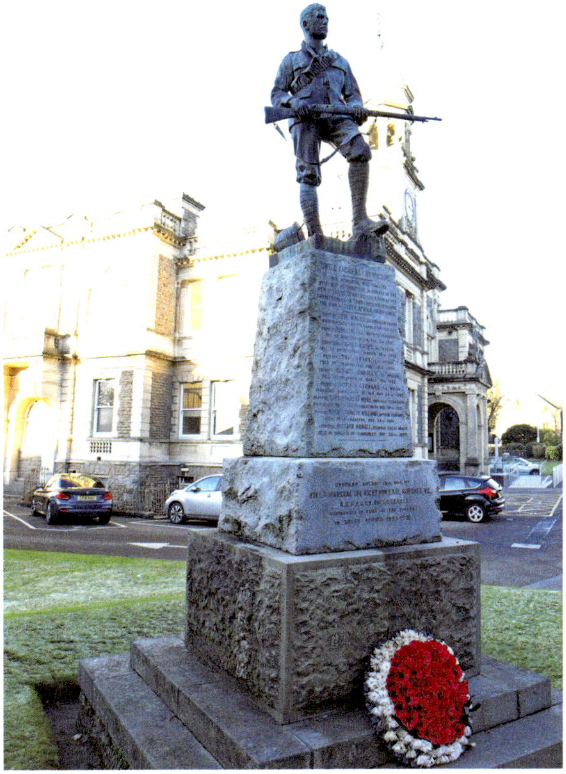

South African War Memorial, Llanelli.

Such were the casualty numbers and carnage created by the First World War (1914–18) that many people called it 'The War to end All Wars'. Communities stripped of their men yearned to preserve the memory of a lost generation in a way never before expressed.

In the absence of government commands, community memorials to the dead of the First World War were commissioned and paid for by public donations and private subscriptions. The style and designs of these memorials are as varied as they are many. Following the Second World War, rather than creating new monuments, it was customary practice to add the names of those who died to existing monuments.

Memorials depicting figures of soldiers were a popular choice, and several fine examples exist in the county. The Pencader war memorial, unveiled on 11 November 1922, depicts an infantry soldier carved from white marble wearing a cloth cap, leaning on a tree stump holding a rifle, and standing on a shell. During the 1950s, a newly polished red-granite base with gold inscriptions was added, remembering seventeen First and four Second World War casualties.

An impressive bronze bareheaded figure of a soldier standing at ease holding his rifle with bayonet fixed stands on a plinth in Priory Street, Carmarthen. The County War Memorial was initially erected to evoke the men of the county who died in the First World War, but now commemorates 1,910 nurses, officers, and men of all ranks from the county who died in both world wars and the Korean War (1950–54).

In Broad Street, Llandovery, a bronze soldier in a greatcoat stands with his head bowed and rifle reversed, as does a white stone soldier in New Street, Kidwelly. Another fashionable style for monuments was the Celtic Cross. A good example can be seen at Pentre Road Bridge, St Clears, which shows those who died in the two world wars and

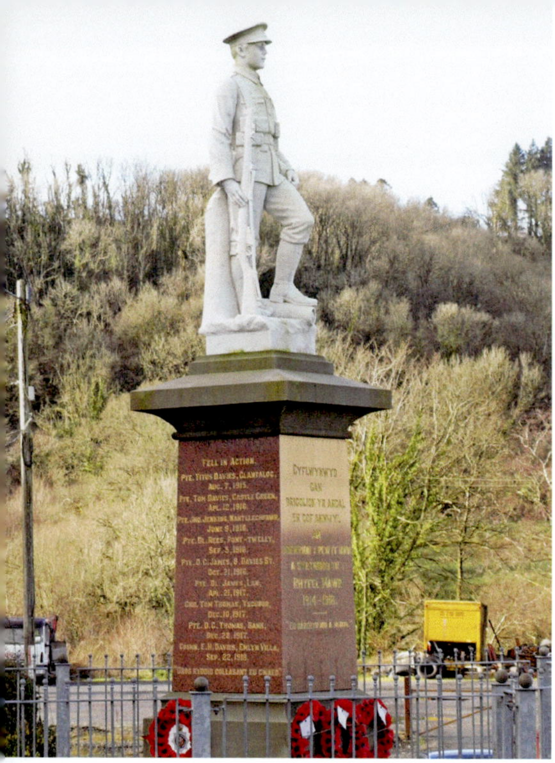

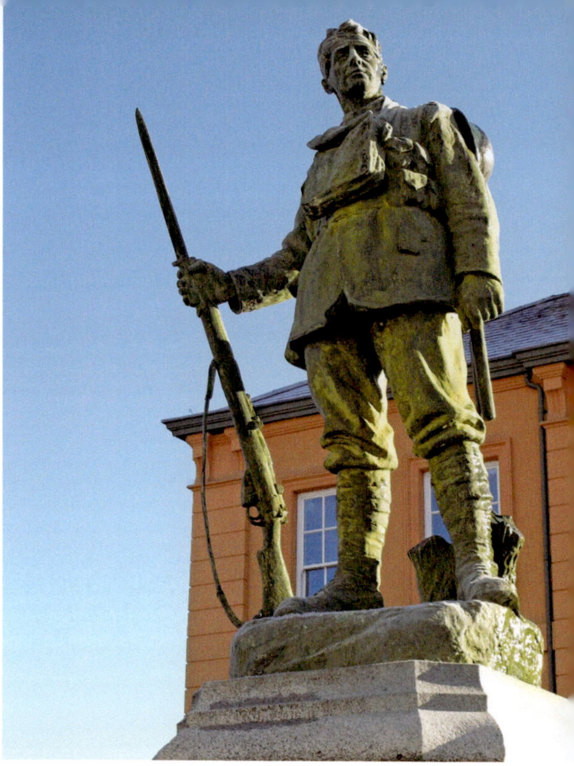

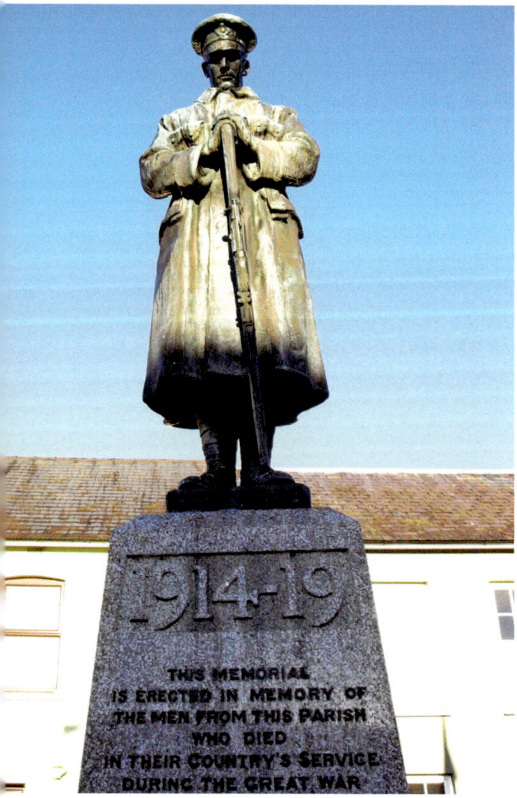

Above left: Pencader War Memorial.

Above right: County War Memorial, Carmarthen.

Left: Llandovery War Memorial.

remembers the local civilians who housed 168 London schoolchildren and twenty-four teachers re-evacuated from Sussex.

One of the more unusual memorials stands at Christ Church, Garnant, and commemorates Mary Doreen Davies or 'Mollie' as she was known. Her father Handel was a mechanic and motorcyclist who served as a dispatch rider on the Western Front throughout the First World War and became a celebrity motor sport star afterwards.

Mollie became a skilled motorcycle rider when she was incredibly young and accompanied her father to racing events around Wales. Following the outbreak of war in 1939, nineteen-year-old Mollie joined the Auxiliary Territorial Service (ATS) as a volunteer. She became a dispatch rider with the Welch Regiment's No. 67 Searchlight Regiment, Territorial Army, at Cardiff. Shortly after qualifying, Mollie contracted pneumonia and died in hospital on 13 February 1940. She was the first ATS female to lose her life during the Second World War. Her family erected a private memorial of a romanticised and resplendent angel, head bowed, holding the limp body of an ATS woman, poised to fly skywards.

The remains of those who died in service during two world wars lie in churchyards throughout the UK and in military cemeteries across Europe and around the world. In keeping with the Commonwealth War Graves Commission's (CWGC) ethos of ensuring each war casualty is commemorated equally, in the UK most of these graves, as in Europe, are marked with an instantly recognisable CWGC headstone made to a standard design and carved from white Portland stone.

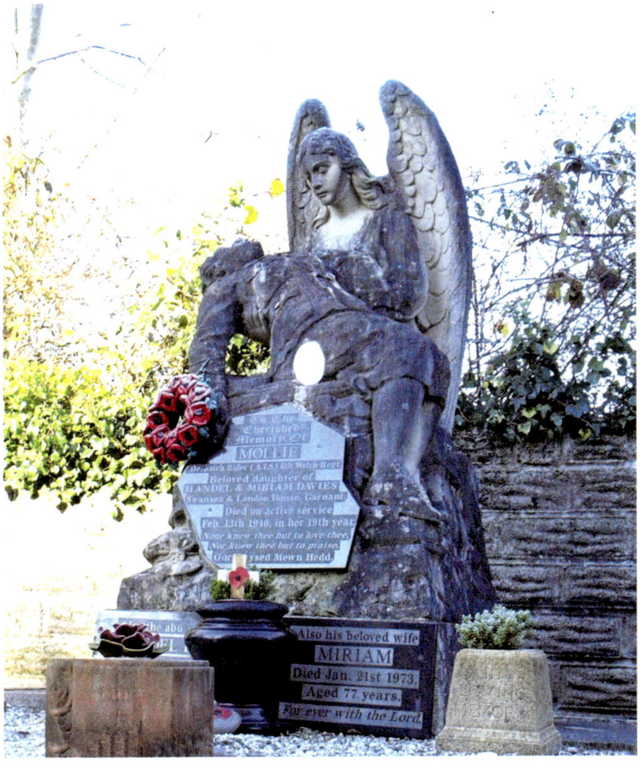

Doreen Davies Monument.

At St Mary's Church, Kidwelly, three headstones made to the standard CWGC design are crafted from black slate, unlike most other churchyards and cemeteries across the county. It is unknown why these graves are marked with slate rather than stone; they remain an interesting and unusual contribution to the county's military heritage.

Two more unusual memorials can be found in the village of Five Roads, where a stone monolith commemorates local casualties from the Boer War, and both world wars. While at Marros a trilithon of Stone Age megaliths dedicate those who died and returned from the First World War.

Besides community remembrance, organisations such as public services, businesses, and schools honoured their employees and membership. At Llanelli, in the old Post Office, St John's Street, a large brass plaque honours nine local postal workers who fell during the First World War. Another brass memorial to postal workers can be found at the Carmarthen delivery office, Stephens Way, Carmarthen. Originally in the now closed King Street Post Office building, it celebrates five postal workers who died during the First World War. A second smaller brass plaque was added later to remember one worker listed as missing during the Second World War.

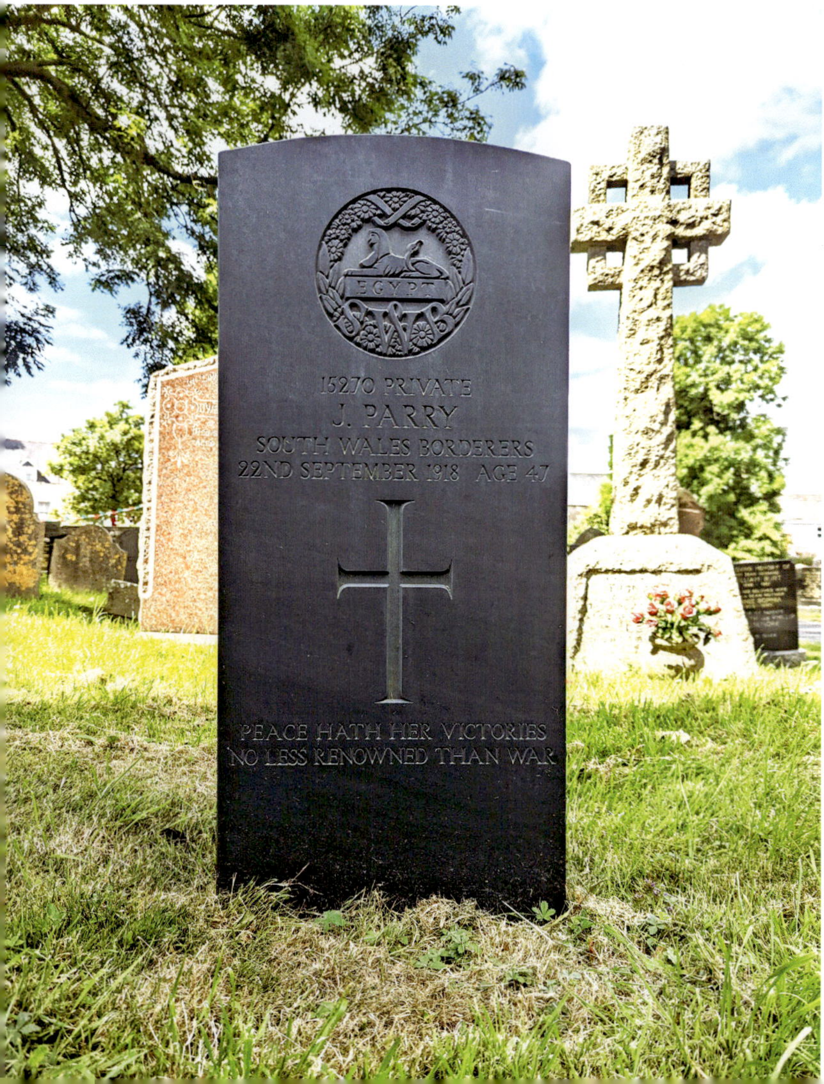

CWGC headstone, St Mary's Church, Kidwelly.

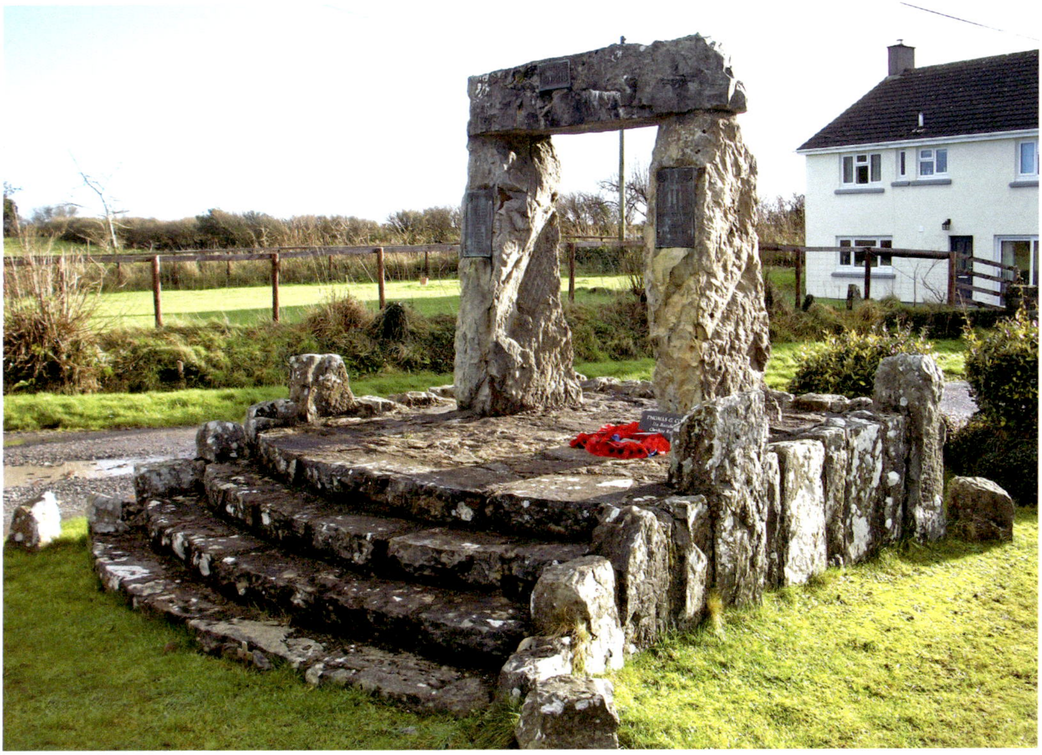

Marros War Memorial.

A wooden roll of honour, once at the former Buckley's Brewery, Llanelli, celebrates the service of thirty members of staff in 1914, men who volunteered to fight during the First World War. Unusually unveiled in February 1915, all thirty men survived. The memorial is now housed at in the Parc Howard Museum, Llanelli.

Another type of tribute was memorial halls, places where military rolls of honour and plaques were located, and people might meet to reflect on their loss. In time they became places of recreation and social interaction. At the Whitland Memorial Hall was constructed in 1927 a large tablet records the names of the fallen in the First World War, along with framed pictures of each servicemember. A second tablet was erected at the end of the Second World War to commemorate the fallen of that war. Each Remembrance Sunday wreaths are laid, and a brief service is held before the parade marches to a local church.

The Llangain and District Memorial Hall holds a plaque containing the names of the seven local men who died in both world wars. The Pontargothi War Memorial Hall is dedicated to ten local men killed during the First World War, while at the Pontyberem Memorial Hall, two brass plaques record fifty-three men killed from both world wars.

In the Burry Port Memorial Hall another brass plaque pays homage to thirty-three Welshmen of the International Brigade who were killed during the Spanish Civil War (1936–39). The International Brigade was military units set up by Communist International to assist the Popular Front government of the Second Spanish Republic, during the Spanish Civil War.

Two other plaques commemorate Carmarthenshire's association with the Spanish Civil War. In the Town Hall, Ammanford, a small brass plaque honours two Amman Valley men who were killed and at Llanelli, outside the Plaid Cymru offices, John Street, a silver plaque names four local men who died in the conflict.

A war memorial with a difference is at the entrance to Ammanford Park, on Iscennen Road, a set of entry gates and stone piers that lead to a tree-lined memorial avenue. In 1937, the Ammanford branch of the British Legion created a memorial featuring a pair of large wrought-iron gates embossed with the words 'Memorial Avenue' and four tall stone piers surmounted by iron lamp stands and glass lamps.

On the right-hand pier marble tablets list the names of eighty-eight men from Ammanford and the surrounding district who died during the First World War. Unusually, the memorial also includes the name of Emma Grace Fletcher, a local nurse who served with the Voluntary Aid Detachment (VAD) in Pontypool Military Hospital. On the left pier similar tablets list the names of forty-two local men who died during the Second World War and each year on Remembrance Sunday, wreaths are laid at the gates.

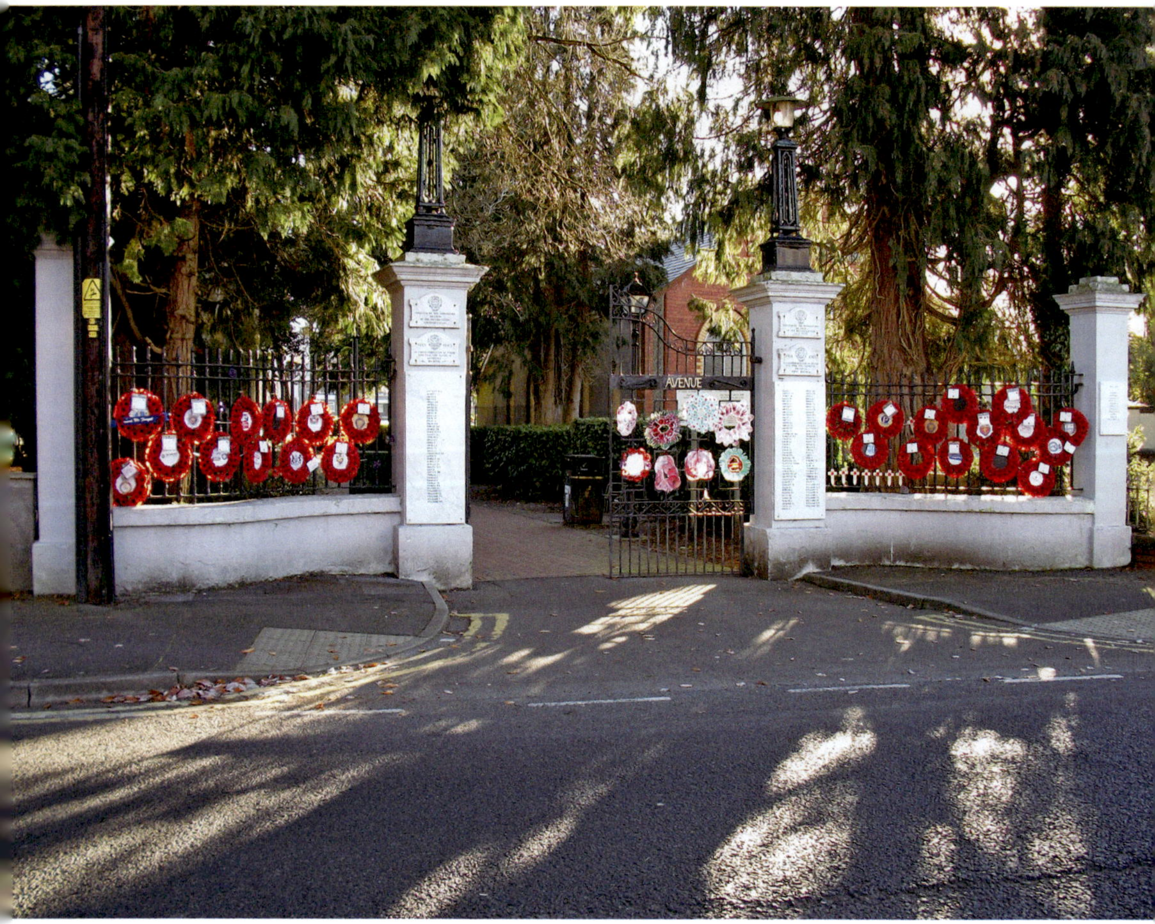

Ammanford War Memorial.

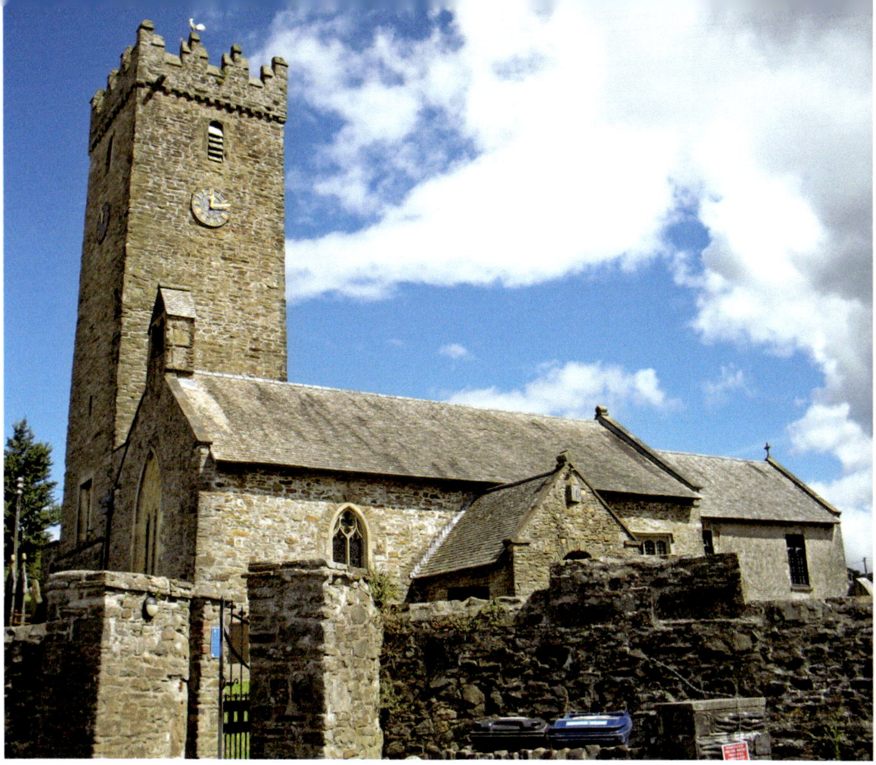

St Illtyd's
Church.

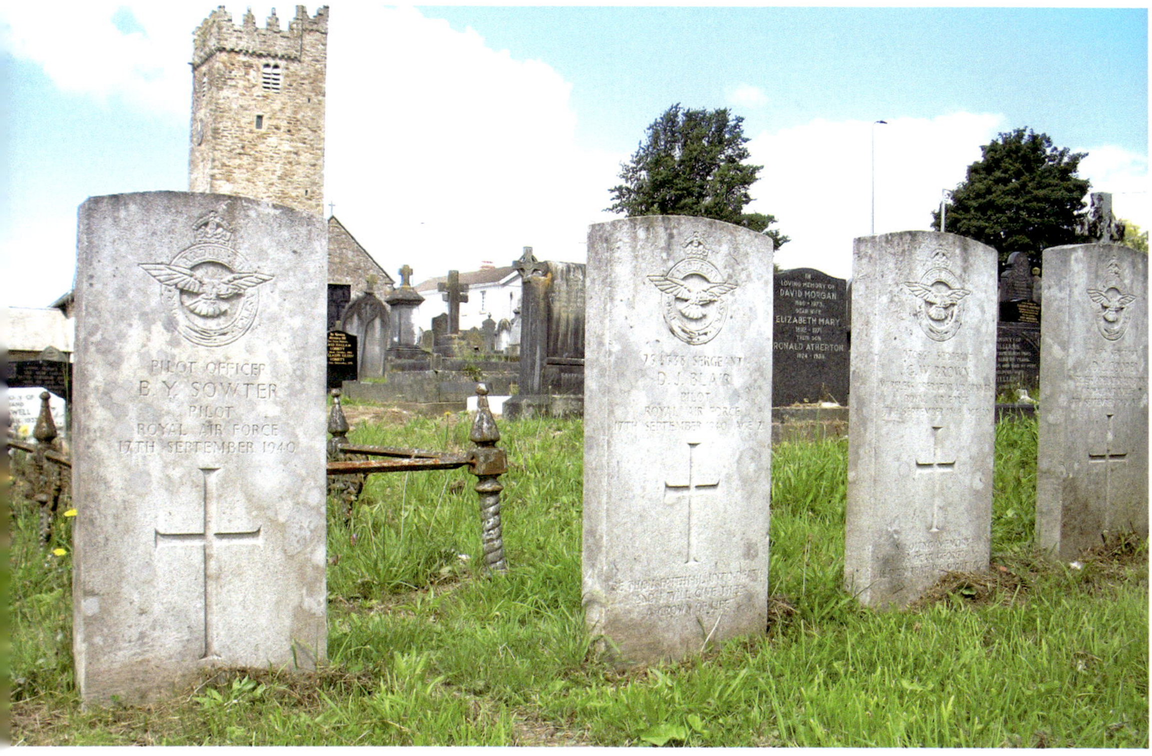

The first four casualties.

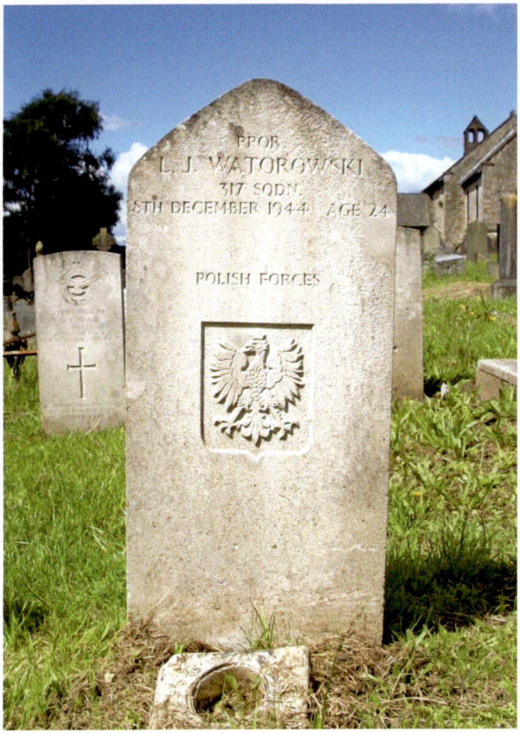

Flying Officer Podporuczn Leon Jan Watorowski.

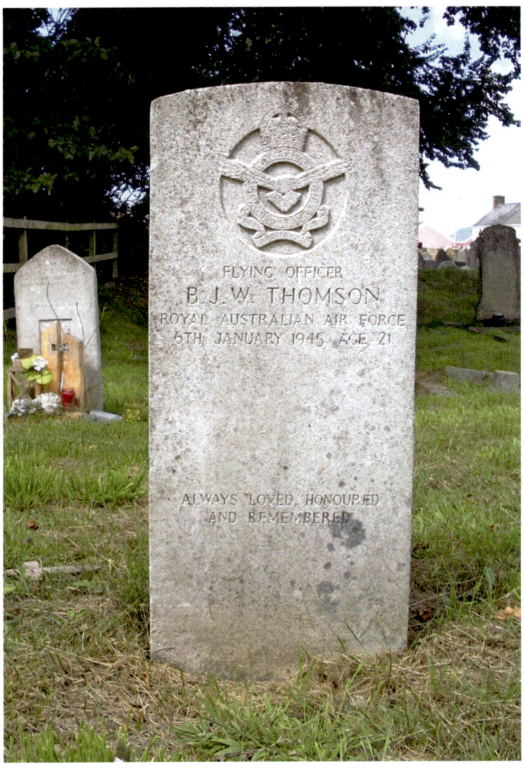

Flying Officer Beverley John Wentworth Thomson.

Acknowledgements

In finding the primary sources needed to research and produce this publication I am thankful and indebted to the many wonderful and like-minded people who I have met along the way. Their help, guidance, generosity, and support as always has proved invaluable. In particular I am thankful to the staff of Carmarthenshire's County Council Library Services and Archives, the staff of Carmarthenshire County Museum and the Llanelli Community Heritage.

For allowing the use of their images I am obliged to:

(ACM) © Arthur Cadwgan Michael (1881–1965) Carmarthenshire County Museum
(AK) © Anna Krivitskaia | Dreamstime.com
(CM) © Colin Moore | Dreamstime.com
(D) © Darrensharvey | Dreamstime.com
(DD) © Dirk Deklein
(FAST) © Farnborough Air Sciences Trust
(HP) © Harry Payne Comitatus re-enactment Group
(JH) © John Hopkins
(LC) © Leighton Collins
(NS) ©Noel Sylvestre Legio VIII Augusta MGV, Roman Living History Society
(PK) © Pavel Kirichenko | Dreamstime.com

All other images are from the author's collection, in the public domain or free from copyright.

I am particularly thankful to John Wynne Hopkins and Andrew Sellick. As always, I offer a special thanks for the continued commendable support afforded me by my wife Maria, for keeping me focussed and allowing me the time to do what I love doing.

Finally, I would like to thank good friends and travel companions Kerry and Storming Norm Goodman whose help, assistance, and support in navigating the county and locating the sites within this book have been invaluable. Last but by no means lest to S. Thomson-Hillis, a most trusted confidant, valued friend, source of encouragement and support and whose truths keep me grounded. Thank you all.

I am also grateful to Amberley Publishing for their continued support and for making my ambitions a reality.

About the Author

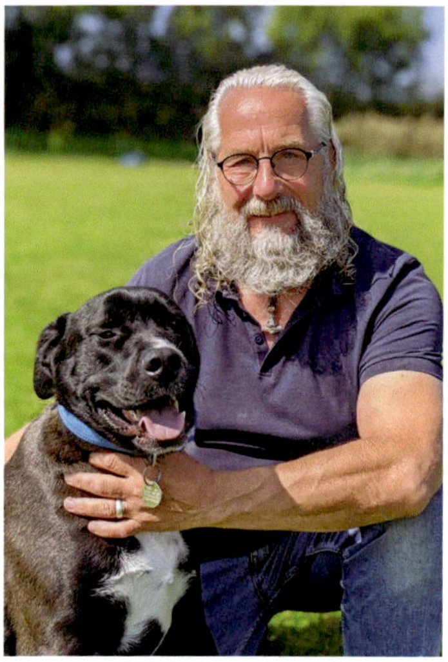

Dean Hollands has had a lifelong interest in military history. Following his father, grandfather, and great-grandfather he joined the army at sixteen, serving with the Royal Army Ordnance Corps for eight years as a Supply Specialist and Physical Training Instructor in the UK, West Germany, and Falkland Islands, attaining the rank of corporal. Following this he joined Surrey Police, retiring as a detective chief inspector after twenty-six years' service. A battlefield and historic sites guide in the UK and Europe, Dean is a member of the Battlefield Trust, Guild of Battlefield Guides, and the Western Front Association.

Dean is regularly invited to speak at national and international conferences about military history and acts as a consultant for the planning and delivery of the New Jersey State Association of Chiefs of Police annual European battlefield staff ride programme in Europe.

Moving to Carmarthenshire in 2021, Dean undertook to write *Carmarthenshire's Military Heritage*, his seventh book in this series, preceded by Hampshire, Kent, Sussex, Farnborough, Berkshire, and Dorset.